"Dean Curry has written a book that is clear, concise, and to the point. In easy to understand language, he spells out who God is, who we are, and what He requires from us. This is something everyone should read, whether believer or unbeliever. I give it my highest recommendation."

— Don Stewart, author of The Final Antichrist

Finale.

Also by Dean Curry:

In the Right Seat

HOPE AM

BOOST!

*52 Infusions of Wisdom to Revolutionize the
Way You Think and Live*

FINALE.

The End Times and Happily Ever After

by Dean Curry

Finale. The End Times and Happily Ever After.

© 2019 Dean Curry

All rights reserved. No portion of this book may be reproduced, stored in a retrieval system, or transmitted in any form or by any means—electronic, mechanical, photocopy, recording, scanning, or other—except for brief quotations in critical reviews or articles, without the prior written permission of the publisher.

Dean Curry

Cover design by Drew Curry

Unless otherwise noted, Scripture quotations are taken from Holy Bible, New Living Translation, © 1996, 2004, 2015 by Tyndale House Foundation. Used by permission of Tyndale House Publishers Inc., Carol Stream, Illinois 60188. All rights reserved.

Scripture quotations marked: **NIV** are from the Holy Bible, New International Version®, NIV®, ©1973, 1978, 1984, 2011 by Biblica, Inc.® Used by permission. All rights reserved worldwide. **MSG** from The Message, © 1993, 1994, 1995, 1996, 2000, 2001, 2002. Used by permission of NavPress Publishing Group. **TLB** from The Living Bible copyright © 1971 by Tyndale House Foundation. Used by permission of Tyndale House Publishers Inc., Carol Stream, Illinois 60188. All rights reserved.

Printed in the United States of America

ISBN: 978-0-9835022-1-0

First Edition

*For my daughter Lauren,
whose questions, hope, and fears ignited my passion for knowing and
explaining the epic resolution of the greatest story ever written.
It's all so wonderfully true.*

*And all those times we'd whisper how much we love each other,
I meant it with all my heart.
You are an answer to actual prayers.*

FINALE

fi·na·le \fə-ˈna-lē, fi-ˈnä-\

the close or termination of something, such as the last and often climactic event or item in a sequence – Merriam Webster[1]

CONTENTS

Prologue 1

What Not to Think 3

Why 9

Weird + Wisdom 25

When & Where 31

Who 43

Whole New World 53

What Now 67

Q & A 79

Notes 85

PROLOGUE

You are living the greatest choose-your-own-adventure chronicle of all time.[1]

Every epic narrative ever imagined emerged from this single true story that has been unfolding since before the beginning.

Author. Hero. Adversary. Battle. Finale.

The battle is about you. You are the prize, the treasure, the heir the enemy wants to take captive whom the Hero will ransom and rescue at any price.

The Author existed before anything and created everything. He wrote you into His story on purpose. He loves you more and has loved you longer than you've ever been or will ever be loved by another. He sacrificed the life of His own Son, the Hero, to save yours. He created you for a forever with Him so wonderful you literally can't imagine it.

The adversary is the original of a familiar cliché: good guy who rose too high and got too greedy. Once one of the Author's most favored, he decided he wanted to be the Author instead. Now he entices allegiants with beguiling lies and half-truths. All who don't choose the Hero, choose the adversary by default.

Every moment, the battle wages. The Hero honorably campaigns for hearts and saves lives. The adversary deceives and discourages, distracts and destructs. Each day the finale draws one day nearer.

The final chapters are already written. The adversary, posing as the Hero, will make a cunning bid for ultimate power and it will look like he has won. But he has lost already, and he knows it. His one kamikaze mission is to destroy as many lives as he can.

The finale isn't the end. It's just the end of everything we know now. After the finale comes forever. And the Author left the choice up to you:

Forever with Him? Or without Him?

You can't even imagine how much He wants you to choose "with Him."

This book is about the coming finale—what we know about it, why it is good news, and why it matters more than many of us think. It's about choosing the Hero who gave His own life for yours, and engaging in the battle for every soul and every forever at stake.

WHAT NOT TO THINK

This is a book about the end times. It's also kind of not.

If you're looking for detailed interpretation of the Bible's symbolic language about the final days on our world's approaching horizon, you won't find it on this page—or the next one, or the one after that.

Instead, here's what you hold in your hand: hope-filled truth from the core of Scripture, spelled out as clearly and simply as I can describe it. Truth that means everything to everyone, whether they know it or not.

I've read more books on the topic of the end times than I ever wanted or thought I needed to. In some ways, I'm still a bit incredulous that I've put my name on one. But (and I know every author thinks or says this), my hope is that you find the ideas you read here to be different than those you've encountered elsewhere. More importantly, I hope they move you to live with perspective and purpose that impacts everyone you encounter and changes lives.

Something has been happening *in* me because of what has been happening *around* me. Repeatedly, I have seen the topic of the end times dominated by hobbyists, false prophets, and profiteers—people who read the front page of the *New York Times* and then try to connect it to first century BC prophecies in order to make money. And people keep buying the books and attending the seminars. This is madness. And it has lit a flame in me.

Perhaps I should mention this now: I like to be candid. It saves all of us time. You won't have to wonder what I'm thinking.

And I'll try to say it in the most loving way.

People who know Jesus ought to be people of hope. It bothers me when I see people who are born into a great inheritance living under oppression and fear. These are people who have the power of Almighty God within them, yet they're fearful of Him coming again.

> People who know Jesus ought to be people of hope.

I am tired of seeing people who are supposed to look forward to Jesus' return as the greatest celebration of all time, instead perceive it as they would a Wes Craven film. As if the book of Revelation was written by Stephen King. Every time some "expert" writes a new book about blood moons or some other phenomenon the Bible never mentions, a fresh wave of speculation and anxiety ripples through the ranks of those who keep a keen eye on this genre.

When it comes to anything connected to the end times, the responses I see most frequently are fascination and fear. Yet neither of these is prescribed in Scripture.

Do you know Jesus? Do you trust Him? Do you believe He is good and He loves you? He tells us not to be afraid, so why are we? He tells us to be busy telling everyone we know who He is and that He loves them, so why aren't we?

HIGH STAKES & FAULTY THINKING

I'm a first generation Jesus person.[1] When I was a young man in third or fourth grade, I was invited to church by a friend. I ended up asking Jesus into my life and becoming part of that church community.

Throughout my younger years, a book by author Hal

Lindsey called *The Late Great Planet Earth* experienced significant popularity.[2] In the early 1980s, Mr. Lindsey came to speak at my church. From the front row to the back of the balcony, every seat was full. People were standing against the walls on the outside aisles. And Hal stood on the stage and stated that Jesus would be coming back—before 1986.

I planned to graduate from high school in 1986. And I can remember sitting in that auditorium thinking, "Oh, no. I'll never get a letterman's jacket."

As it turned out, Jesus didn't come before 1986. I got my letterman's jacket and graduated from high school. Hal Lindsey sold a bunch of books and wrote some more. But there was no Second Coming.

In 1987 another end times book, *88 Reasons Why the Rapture will be in 1988*,[3] was launched into circulation. Recently, I wondered if there were still any copies still available for sale, so I looked it up on Amazon.com. Not only is it still available, but over the last decade a dozen readers have taken the time to write reviews. Here are a few:

> "This book really stands the test of time. Looking back, the world clearly ended on September 11, 1988 and everything since has been an illusion. I highly recommend this book for anyone who loves irony. Want more irony? Mr Whisenant died in May of 2001, just a few months before 9/11, a golden opportunity to froth about the end times again."

> "When I was around 7, my parents had this book. It sat on the coffee table, scaring the bejesus out of me. I had forgotten about it, but thanks for the reminder of why I have generalized anxiety disorder."

> "I too was one of the idiots who bought into this hysteria

> in 1988. I was a naive 21 year old who put way too much faith into anything my church pastor taught. When he brought Edgar Whisenant to our church for a series of talks about the 88 reasons, I believed every word because my pastor believed it. As a matter of fact, belief in this book compelled my then girlfriend and I to marry much earlier than we originally had intended. We were taught that what is bound together on earth will be bound together in heaven and so we HAD to get married so we would be together after the rapture occurred. When the designated range of dates passed, I remember there being a lot of confusion and anger in the church and we ended up leaving. After several years of religious exploration dosed with much more skepticism than before, my wife and I both ended up rejecting Christianity all together. I'm not saying that his book caused us to become atheists, but it was a major catalyst for us to start thinking for ourselves about religious issues. In light of that and its novelty value now, I give it 5 stars. Oh, and we just celebrated our 25th wedding anniversary!"[4]

The end times are a high stakes conversation. Yet so many Jesus people treat them like novelty. We need to use our brains about these things. But so often we don't.

A family member once called to tell me he was sure the Second Coming was on the horizon because he had gotten a credit card in the mail with the last three digits 666. So he cancelled the credit card. In fact, he cancelled all his credit cards, told me he would never get another credit card, and was sure the expiration date on the card he had received was an indicator of when Jesus was going to come.

I give you this brief, rather ironic introduction to illustrate why I take this seriously. As I've already mentioned, it bugs me a ton that Jesus people are so afraid about the end times. Jesus' promised return is our blessed hope. We are supposed to look forward to that day, not dread it.

If you've ever played sports, you know that if you're ahead in the game, you want the clock to keep ticking. It's only when you're down a few points that you're hoping the clock stops. I believe the enemy is dreading the end, but we should be tickled about it. Because we win.

Maybe you are looking forward to Jesus' return with unreserved anticipation. Or maybe you're one of the many who are fearful about the end times. Either way, my one goal here is to replace some of the misdirected thinking and feeling about this topic with clarity, and hopefully some calm and confidence as well. Not by giving you my opinion or someone else's, but by starting with the words of Jesus.

Full disclosure: I will share some opinions and personal conclusions along the way. And I'll be careful to identify these as my own ideas rather than the words of Scripture. Receive them or don't receive them. Agree with them or don't agree. Consider them or don't. But at least we will have talked and thought about something that matters—not just for today, but for all time.

WHY?

Why is the end times a topic of interest for so many? Perhaps because it's combustible. In chemistry terms, if something is stable, it's boring. Nobody worries about carrying water around. H2O is pretty stable. But there are other solutions you have to handle with extreme care. If they get a little shaken up or collide with something else, a massive explosion happens. And that's kind of exciting, isn't it? The element of the unknown, the potential for danger or damage.

I think this is what appeals to a lot of people about the idea of the end times—both the biblical version and the world's myriad imaginary ones. Apocalypse. Armageddon. The book writers have written countless books, and the movie-makers have made countless movies, about one end-of-the-world scenario after another. Without fail, the books fly off the shelves and the theaters fill each time a new one is released.

Perhaps you're a scholar of what the Bible says about the end times. You've been to a prophecy seminar or several. You've got end times books on your book shelves. This is an area of interest for you.

I'll be honest: I am not of the same mind. The end times are not a hobby for me. The details of this topic are not central to my everyday thinking. That's why when the Holy Spirit directed me to allocate several weekends to talk about this to my church community, and months later nudged me to put those talks into the book you hold in your hand, I knew I had a unique assignment.

The world doesn't really need one more ultra-nuanced talk or book about blood moons or weather patterns or natural disasters, does it? Or another highly studied, extensively supported interpretation of end times prophecy. There are plenty of them out there, and you'll find a list of some I highly recommend in the last chapter of this book. But the pages you're reading now are the end result of a different approach.

If you've been to an end times seminar, think for a moment about the experience. Most prophetic teachers are about teaching you what to think. They do the interpretation for you because they are the experts. They say, "This is what the prophecy says, and here's what it means." Has that been your experience with teaching on this topic?

I'll tell you up front: I am not a prophetic teacher. Nor am I an expert on interpreting prophecy. In fact, at perhaps the complete opposite end of the spectrum, I was a philosophy major in college. There is a radical difference in how a philosophy teacher approaches an idea, versus those who teach in other subject areas.

For instance, math, science, history, or literature professors teach you facts, methods, and perspectives in their respective areas of expertise. A professor has a point of view and uses his or her position to download it to you. Frequently, after a certain amount of study under a person's teaching, you end up thinking much the same way he or she does in relation to that particular subject. This occurs because most people who consider themselves students place themselves in a position of being taught what to think.

Here's the contrast. When you study philosophy, the professors don't teach you *what* to think. They teach you *how* to think. The difference is a fundamental one that produces profoundly different learning outcomes. Which is why this book will hopefully be very different than any other you may have read or may yet read on the end times.

I'm not here to teach you what to think. Instead, this book is my effort to teach you *to* think, and *how* to think, about the end times. It's not my intent to be cryptic or cagey. If you ask me a question, I will tell you what I think and why I think it. But frankly, I don't want you to take my word for it. I want you to read the Bible, think about what you read and how it fits with what else you know about Jesus, and listen to what the Holy Spirit tells you about all of it.

And when you decide what you think about it, I'll challenge what you think and you can challenge what I think. But until we both learn how to think, and are willing to think, it's not very helpful for me to just talk about what I think. After all, what if I'm wrong? Unless you study and think for yourself, neither of us will ever know.

So one "why" of this book is to encourage you to think, and to give you some ideas about where to start looking, how to start thinking about this topic, and how to live with it in mind.

One of the longtime challenges of studying the end times is that the Bible's description is enigmatic. Anyone who tries to tell you it's all crystal clear is not speaking the truth. Some of it is plainly presented and seems straightforward. Other statements are so general or figuratively indistinct that they could be applied to a number of specific events or situations.

When things are clear, we don't even have to think about what to think. The Bible tells us. For me, the Bible is authoritative. So where it requires no interpretation, I simply believe what it says.

However, in the places where it's unclear what Scripture is specifically referring to, I'm most interested in talking about how to think. These are places where the Bible tells us, sometimes explicitly, that wisdom is required. We want to be careful how we think—not just to get to a conclusion, but to think through things so we're enriched regardless of what our conclusion is.

Lastly, in addition to approaching this topic from a philosophical perspective, I'm a reductionist. Meaning, when I explain something, I try to put it in its simplest form. I believe mastery of any topic gives one the ability to say things simply. This doesn't mean I think everything is simple. It means that I try to explain complicated things in a simple way.

Maybe you'd like to talk about this topic for hours and explore every detail. I have no doubt you can find people who want to have that conversation. But the job I think I've been given is to equip people for the world they're living in. I'm not trying to impress you with what or how much I know. I'm simply offering you the truth and tools I have. My hope is that you will use them to engage this world with confidence, and explain these things simply to someone who needs to understand them.

WHY DO THE END TIMES MATTER?

Did you know the topic of the end times is blessed? John writes in the book of Revelation:

> *"God blesses the one who reads the words of this prophecy to the church, and he blesses all who listen to its message and obey what it says, for the time is near."*[1]

There's so much hope here, so much blessing, so much potential. It troubles me greatly that so many Jesus people are missing it. The enemy wants you to be afraid of Jesus' coming, not look forward to it with assurance and peace. So he distracts and divides Jesus people over minor details and inconsequential arguments. I don't want you to miss this blessing that's just waiting for you to claim it.

I also believe the end times matter because Jesus says they do. I'm a Jesus guy and His words weigh a lot with me. With any topic I speak on, I always try to include some of the words of Jesus. Here's what He said about His own coming:

> *"Be dressed for service and keep your lamps burning, as though you were waiting for your master to return from the wedding feast. Then you will be ready to open the door and let him in the moment he arrives and knocks. The servants who are ready and waiting for his return will be rewarded."*[2]

Pay attention to the word "rewarded" in the Bible. It's there a ton. Sometimes we act like heaven is a youth hostel in the middle of Europe where nobody owns anything and nobody gets anything and you're just grateful to have a room. No! The Bible talks all the time about rewards in heaven. I'm telling you, this Second Coming thing is fabulous for Jesus people. I'm ready. I'm waiting. I'm working. And I'm looking forward to blessings.

> *"I tell you the truth, he himself will seat them, put on an apron, and serve them as they sit and eat!"*[3]

This is what the Master is going to do. He is going to bless people Himself. He's not going to have other people do it.

The end times matter because Jesus says they do.

Right now I'm blessing you in Jesus' name. Perhaps other people have also blessed you in Jesus' name. Hopefully you are blessing people in His name. But let's pause for a moment and take in the thought that there is a day coming when Jesus will be speaking for Himself and we will be listening to Him together. I cannot wait for the day when I can simply sit and listen and hear Him talk. About all the stories the Bible only tells us part of. About all the stories in our own lives we didn't understand because we could only see our own part.

> "'He may come in the middle of the night or just before dawn. But whenever he comes, he will reward the servants who are ready.'"[4]

(Did you catch the word "reward" again?)

> "'Understand this: If a homeowner knew exactly when a burglar was coming, he would not permit his house to be broken into. You also must be ready all the time, for the Son of Man will come when least expected.'
>
> "Peter asked, 'Lord, is that illustration just for us or for everyone?'"[5]

Peter was trying to figure out, "Who are you talking to? Is this us? Are you telling us we're not ready or we should be more ready? Or are you talking to other people?"

> "And the Lord replied, 'A faithful, sensible servant is one to whom the master can give the responsibility of managing his other household servants and feeding them. If the master returns and finds that the servant has done a good job, there will be a reward. I tell you the truth, the master will put that servant in charge of all he owns. But what if the servant thinks...'"[6]

In my Bible, I always circle thought words. I have the word "thinks" circled here, because if you start thinking wrong, it's only a matter of time until you're afraid of something you should be happy about, and you're happy about something you should be afraid of.

> "'..."My master won't be back for a while," and he begins beating the other servants, partying, and getting drunk? The master will return unannounced and unexpected, and he will cut the servant in pieces and banish him with the unfaithful.
>
> "'And a servant who knows what the master wants, but

isn't prepared and doesn't carry out those instructions, will be severely punished.'"[7]

We have two different types of servants here. One guy is drunk and partying and doing whatever he pleases, so he doesn't expect his master's return and he's unprepared. The other guy expects it, but he's unprepared. Both are in trouble.

"'But someone who does not know, and then does something wrong, will be punished only lightly. When someone has been given much, much will be required in return; and when someone has been entrusted with much, even more will be required.'"[8]

Many of us have heard the words of Luke 12:48: "*When someone has been given much, much will be required in return.*" But did you know the context had to do with the end times? In essence, Jesus' response to Peter's question is this: "Yes, you have an extra responsibility."

You are blessed with opportunity and information. You're also blessed with a responsibility.

There are people in Iran who have been acquainted with Jesus for only a few weeks and don't yet understand what they have to look forward to. These people are in the category of *"someone who does not know."* Their mantle of responsibility is significantly lighter.

Conversely, in America, where I'm writing this and where it will likely be most read, we have the freedom to read, study, think, talk and even meet about these things. If we're American citizens, we have had that freedom our entire lives. We've had books in our public libraries and Bibles and teaching in our churches every weekend. You don't need a dime or a license to hear or talk about Jesus in America. If you're reading this, and especially if you finish it, you are in the category of someone who *"has been given much"* and *"entrusted with much."* You are blessed that you have the opportunity to be informed about the end times. You're also blessed with a responsibility—to expect Jesus' return, look forward to it, and prepare for it as He told us to.

So what does Jesus mean when He says, *"what the master wants,"* and refers to being prepared and carrying out instructions? He's not talking about stockpiling food or having extra batteries for when the bomb goes off. Jesus was not a survivalist. He isn't trying to get you to survive. He's trying to get you to share your faith. He's not trying to preserve your body. He is not working to preserve the boundaries and the sovereignty of your country. He is working to expand His kingdom, and His kingdom is people.

This is why we've got to think about this. The Big Why is Jesus. This whole thing is centered around Jesus. Not the antichrist. Not an atomic bomb. I've heard that ISIS has enough nuclear material to make a dirty bomb. That's interesting. I'm glad we have people protecting us. But ISIS isn't central to the end times. Jesus is central. The carpenter from Nazareth. It's His party. He came the first time. He's coming the second time. Our job is to be ready, earnestly doing the work He entrusted to us, working to bring as many people into His kingdom as we can.

WHY WAIT?

I believe, as the disciples did, that history and the world are poised for the finale. No other prophesied events need to occur for Jesus to gather His church from the earth to join Him in heaven, and for the season of "great tribulation" to begin.[9] In fact, the three major things Jesus promised would happen before His return had already happened in the disciples' lifetime:

- Jesus stated that the temple in Jerusalem would be destroyed. That happened in 70 A.D.

- He said the gospel had to be preached around the world. As soon as the gospel began being shared with the Gentiles, the disciples and believers felt this prophecy had been fulfilled.

- Lastly, Jesus said difficulty, distress, and tribulation were going to happen to the church. The disciples knew from firsthand experience that had already begun.

By 70 A.D. the church was ready and anticipating Jesus' return. His disciples lived with this urgency in mind, and Jesus people have been doing the same ever since.

The question here isn't, "Will it happen?" or, "When will it happen?" The question is, "Why hasn't it happened yet?"

The answer is in Peter's second letter to the church:

> *"Most importantly, I want to remind you that in the last days scoffers will come, mocking the truth and following their own desires. They will say, 'What happened to the promise that Jesus is coming again? From before the times of our ancestors, everything has remained the same since the world was first created.' They deliberately forget that God made the heavens long ago by the word of his command,"*[10]

This is important because everything was created by God's word and everything is changing by His word. The end times move forward when He says so. The presidents of nations are not in charge of the end times. The devil is not in charge of the end times. Only when God says it is time will these events be set in motion.

"*and he brought the earth out from the water and surrounded it with water. Then he used the water to destroy the ancient world with a mighty flood. And by the same word, the present heavens and earth have been stored up for fire.*

"*They are being kept for the day of judgment, when ungodly people will be destroyed. But you must not forget this one thing, dear friends: A day is like a thousand years to the Lord, and a thousand years is like a day. The Lord isn't really being slow about his promise, as some people think. No, he is being patient for your sake. He does not want anyone to be destroyed, but wants everyone to repent.*"[11]

This is the fundamental "why" the end times haven't happened yet. Jesus is waiting for more people to know Him.

I met Jesus when I was twelve. Let's say it was in 1980, give or take a few years. Did you meet Jesus and stake your life on Him between 1980 and today? How many people do you know who have? Aren't you glad He waited for you and/or them? Yeah. Me, too.

Jesus is waiting so that everybody you know has a chance to know Him. I am so glad that when I became a Jesus person someone hadn't checked out already. That somebody hadn't decided, "Our church is fine exactly the way it is." They did have a nice church before I showed up. And maybe your church was a pretty nice place before you showed up, too.

The end times move forward when God says so.

But you know what? If you're a Jesus follower, I hope you and I are doing things now that weren't happening in our churches before we came on the scene. If you're not, and I say this with love, it's time for you to start. At my church, we keep doing what we're doing—whether it's a community-wide event once a year, or a helping hand once a month, or a Bible study at a coffee shop tomorrow morning—because more people need Jesus. If you want to expedite the end times, here's what you do: You walk next door and ask your neighbor if he or she wants to have coffee. And you sit down with them and say, "Tell me your story. Are you a spiritual person?" That's how we prepare for Jesus' return, and how we bring it a little closer.

WHY RETURN?

The Bible tells us Jesus is in heaven, seated next to God and ruling with Him.[12] Why would He return to earth at all? Because Jesus has a bride, and she is the church. If you're part of the church—if you're among the millions around the world who have chosen the life and freedom Jesus offers—He's coming for you.

Isn't it cool when you find out somebody goes to a lot of trouble for you? When my kids reached the age of around fourteen, my wife and I stopped giving them presents. Stuff breaks, but memories last. So we started saving up our money and giving them experiences instead of stuff. When my daughter turned twenty-one, I had a bunch of air miles saved up so we surprised her with a trip to Arizona for a couple of days. The tears on her face when she saw the effort invested for her are still fresh in my mind.

Yes, Jesus is waiting for more people to be saved. He's also waiting so they, too, can share what those of us who know Him have already experienced. There's an epic love story unfolding that is far more vast and complex than we can imagine, complete with battles and honor and sacrifice. Even when we read the entire Bible, we catch a mere glimpse of the full narrative. Jesus is masterminding and orchestrating the entire thing. For you and me. Because He loves us. Inexplicably. Passionately and patiently. Unswervingly. Purposefully.

He has a plan. And He will not leave His bride waiting at the altar.

WHY AN ANTICHRIST?

Why an antichrist? It's an interesting question. My answer is Genesis. In the beginning, in Eden, the devil approached the first two people God ever created and posed a question: Could it be that God doesn't want you to be His equal?[13] In fact, we learn later in Scripture that this storyline goes back even farther, to when he himself was cast out of heaven. Lucifer, who once held one of the highest positions of favor and responsibility in heaven, was evicted because he began thinking of himself as an equal with God.[14]

The storyline of the antichrist is that he will resolve a great problem here on earth and be celebrated for three and a half years. But recognition, accomplishment, and power won't be enough for him. (Do you see the parallel?) At that three and a half year mark, he will proclaim himself to be the king and put in place what is called the abomination of desolation.[15] He will walk into the temple in Jerusalem and say, "I'm not just a great diplomat. I am God." And then, through the events described in the book of Revelation, we will see the final resolution of what began in the book of Genesis.

WHY CARE?

Why should you care about the end times? To me, this is the most important topic in eternity. Certainly the most important topic in history.

History is not circular. History is linear. It's going somewhere. History had a beginning and the Bible teaches that history will have an end.

I believe Jesus really did come to earth as a man. He really did die on a cross. He really did come out of a grave. I believe He is coming again. I believe every prophecy predicted to happen before Jesus' return has happened. I believe every person on earth needs Jesus. I believe eternity is for real and we're all going toward it. And I think it's very confusing to the world when followers of Jesus live as if life is going to go on forever and what we believe is not consequential.

The Bible says what your faith is matters. If you don't know Jesus, it matters. If you reject Jesus, it matters. If you know Jesus but don't tell anyone else about Him, it matters. Jesus came and died for every Hindu, every Muslim, every atheist, every agnostic. He's not just Episcopalian. Jesus isn't a Baptist. Jesus is for everybody. Everybody.

I want to remind you that your here-and-now isn't the only thing happening.

Marcus Aurelius, the great Roman emperor, employed a unique strategy in an attempt to cultivate humility among his leaders throughout the empire. During his reign near the end of what is known as Pax Romana, the Roman Empire was vast and powerful. Victories were frequent, and celebration was effusive. History tells us that when a conquering general returned home from winning a battle, the roads would be lined with people cheering the glory of Rome and this great Roman hero. Each time, Marcus Aurelius would order the placement of a servant behind the conquering general to whisper a single sentence over and over again: "Memento mori. Memento mori." It just means, "Remember, you're only a man. Remember, one day you will die." There's something about the reminder that this life is coming to an end, and that history is marching toward a conclusion, that puts things in perspective.

If you are a follower of Jesus today, you can look forward to the certainty of heaven. But here's my "Memento mori" to you: I beg you to never lose sight of the fact that what Jesus did—what He came to earth to do for you and for everyone you love—is eternally, permanently, absolutely consequential.

I believe it's consequential that you're reading this page today. Everywhere in our world, people are living and dying, desperate, addicted. People you love. Yet so many who know Jesus are holding inside them the truth about who Jesus is. Frankly, I have no understanding of why a follower of Jesus would not tell other people about Him. If you're a Jesus person, are you telling other people about Him? If not, why aren't you? To protect your reputation? To be honest, your reputation isn't that awesome. How could it possibly be worth the cost of somebody else's eternity?

If Jesus really was who He said He was, and we believe the Bible when it says time will come to an end, then we need to be living with a sense of urgency. I'm not playing religious games. The world doesn't need more religion. The world is drowning in religion. What the world needs is love and peace and transcendent moments with the living God. It doesn't need Protestantism. It doesn't Catholicism. It doesn't need "isms." It needs to know that Jesus is alive and breathing and He wants to do something significant through you. If you are just another person playing religious games, you are wasting your time.

Why care about the end times? I care because I care about the people I meet every day who don't know Jesus yet. And the ones I don't meet, but you do. Do you have a sense of urgency for the lost? Have you ever introduced someone to Jesus?

It troubles me how many followers of Jesus have never led one other person to Him. I've met, talked with, and lived life alongside a staggering number of people who consider themselves followers of Jesus. So many of them live for Jesus, love Jesus, need Jesus, pray to Jesus, sing songs about Jesus, read books about Jesus, maybe even attend prophetic seminars about Jesus. Yet the vast majority have lockjaw when it comes to telling anybody how He has changed their life.

If more people who know Jesus would start talking about Him, the potential is profound—for churches, for communities, for countries, for our world, and most importantly, for eternity. Just think about the math. If every follower of Jesus introduced one person to Him every three years, the church would double, exponentially, every three years. In most churches, this is not happening. But can you imagine the math for the kingdom if, in every thousand days, every Jesus person helped one person who doesn't know Jesus begin a new relationship with Him?

Multiplication is totally different than addition. Two plus two equals four. Plus another two equals six. Plus another two equals eight. But two *times* two equals four. Times another two is eight. Times another two is sixteen. Pretty soon we are into some very significant numbers. The kingdom is about multiplication. And we have to be, too.

Why would I write a book about the end times, and why would you read it? Why do the end times matter? Why should we care?

Because eternity is on the horizon and lives are at stake.

WEIRD + WISDOM

It's all weird.

An important acknowledgment to make about what Scripture tells us about the end times is that it's all weird. I'm not kidding. It's all weird in the sense that it's all supernatural.

Here's how the dictionary defines weird:

> *"involving or suggesting the supernatural; unearthly or uncanny; that which is mysterious and apparently outside natural law."*[1]

By that definition, the entire Bible is weird. Because it's not just about flesh and blood, the earth, and everything we can see and touch. It is about the mystery of a God who is all powerful, all loving, and all knowing. A God who has been and still is orchestrating a bigger and more complex story than any of us can fully grasp, on a timeline longer than we can fathom.

In order to approach what Scripture says about the end times, we've got to get comfortable with the idea that the Bible assumes an expanded plane of reality. One that includes not only the physical, but also the *meta*physical—a reality beyond what is perceptible to the senses.[2]

I'm considered a moderate in the Christian world. But in the opinion of those who consider themselves experts in the intellectual realms of our culture, anybody who believes in something they can't put in a test tube belongs in the category of weird. Whether you are the most conservative follower of Jesus possible, or the most flamboyant advocate and pursuer of His supernatural power, anyone and everyone on the spectrum of following Jesus is categorically weird. Because we believe God became a flesh-and-blood man who worked as a carpenter. He knew the thoughts of God because He was God. He died like a criminal, but He came out of the grave. He was literally dead for three days, and He came back to life again.

> The entire message of the Bible is that there is more going on than meets the eye.

Do you believe that? I believe it. I'm not only banking my life on it, I'm banking my eternity on it. The entire message of the Bible—including its content about the end times—is that there is more going on at all times than what meets the eye.

SOME OF IT IS WEIRD

When we look at the broad scope of material and discussion about the end times, not all of it is weird because it is supernatural. There's a substantial amount of thinking that is weird because it is untethered to Scripture. One of the factors that prompted me to spend time and money talking and writing about this topic is that for too long I have been hearing too many ideas posed about the end times that are not anchored in the inspired Word of God. These are stirring up confusion and misunderstanding, worry and division. That's a weird I can't live with.

If you're a follower of Jesus, please hear me on this. We can't abide weirdness around this topic or any other topic that is not directly linked to Scripture. Let's absolutely acknowledge that we believe in the supernatural, but let's be careful to tie our metaphysical beliefs to Scripture alone. I don't believe Jesus came back from the dead because I kind of like the idea. I believe it because I have found the Bible to be true and that's what the Bible says. Because of who I know Jesus to be, when God's word says it, I believe it.

Without question, the end times dialogue will always be a discussion involving the weird. But when the weird isn't tethered to Scripture and Jesus, it is not worth my time or yours.

SPECIFICALLY WEIRD

Lastly, there are certain aspects of the end times discussion that inarguably appear in Scripture, but are specifically weird because they have been plucked out of the narrative and magnified. More than once in discussions about the end times, I have found myself saying, "Yes, that's in Scripture. But you are making it weirder than it needs to be."

The number 666 is one such example. Three verses in Revelation are basically the sum total of what Scripture says about this number, yet in my experience almost every discussion about the antichrist gravitates there almost immediately. In fact, some people have elevated that number to such significance that they go to great lengths to avoid it. They are convinced of supernatural significance wherever they encounter it: on a credit card number sequence, a receipt, an account number, a hotel room, a street address, etc.

What the Bible says about the end times—and about any topic Scripture addresses—is intended to be studied as a whole body of information. Picking and choosing parts of the story to put under a microscope and magnify independently is not going to lead to understanding. It's going to yield a fundamentally altered perspective that is disconnected from its full context.

WISDOM IS NEEDED

Let's juxtapose this discussion of the weird with a dozen words in the book of Revelation I think are often overlooked. We find them in chapter 16:

> "He required everyone—small and great, rich and poor, free and slave—to be given a mark on the right hand or on the forehead. And no one could buy or sell anything without that mark, which was either the name of the beast or the number representing his name. **Wisdom is needed here. Let the one with understanding solve the meaning** of the number of the beast, for it is the number of a man. His number is 666."[3]

I know those words aren't in bold face type in your Bible. They aren't in mine, either. But I have highlighted them as a reminder that wisdom and understanding are needed when it comes to "solving the meaning" of the Bible's language about the end times. These passages and prophecies are undeniably a complex puzzle—a fantastic blend of the literal and the figurative, laid out on a timeline and a map that are drawn in units we can only guess at.

Consider the larger passage that includes these three verses. It talks about two beasts (one of them with multiple heads) and a dragon, and a fatal wound that had been miraculously healed. It's weird when you read about it on the page, and it gets even weirder when people start trying to interpret it through the lens of current events and people in positions of leadership around the world.

Wisdom is needed. We need to be people of understanding as we approach this topic. I don't claim to understand every detail of what Scripture says about it, and I don't deny that studying it is challenging. The sheer volume of conjectural material on the end times and the scope of ideas posited are daunting. As a result, I've seen too many capable, intelligent, Jesus-loving people discouraged from even approaching it and doubt their ability to correctly understand it.

> If it's in God's word, I believe He wants us to know it and the Holy Spirit can help us understand it.

If it's in God's word, I believe He wants us to know it and the Holy Spirit can help us understand it. Jesus Himself talked to His disciples about the end times more than once and used a variety of illustrations. Both the disciples' questions and Jesus' answers are recorded for us by multiple authors. Angels and visions were sent to Daniel, Ezekiel, and John with instructions to write down what they saw for the generations to come. If God invested that much intention and direction in placing this information in Scripture—in the specific language and imagery in which it appears—to me, that communicates importance and merits my attention.

WHEN & WHERE

Have you heard of the Doomsday Clock? Since the 1940s, a group of researchers has maintained this symbolic "clock" as a representative indicator of the likelihood of global catastrophe. It is periodically advanced or turned back in accordance with the perceived level of threat. As of this writing, the hands of the Doomsday Clock are poised at two minutes to "midnight."[1]

This is a secular point of view about something catastrophic. It has nothing to do with the metaphysical. But it demonstrates that even the secular world has been in a season of anticipating "the end" for some time.

The end times actually began when God sent His Son to a teenage girl. The first appearance of Jesus on earth was the beginning of the end of life as we know it. And when He first appeared, it was a good thing.

> **The end times are both prelude and finale to the second arrival of the best thing this world has ever seen: the Prince of Peace.**

I want to encourage you. The end times are both prelude and finale to the second arrival of the best thing this world has ever seen: the Prince of Peace. If you're reading this and you're not a Jesus person, I hope that somewhere on these pages you'll find a reason to believe you need to explore who He is. He did not come as a ghoul or a zombie to scare you into making some confession. He came as a loving friend who cared about you before you even knew

His name.

If you want to begin studying the end times, you could dive into the Bible in a lot of different places. Almost every book in the New Testament references the end times. In fact, an average of one in every twenty-five verses of the New Testament has an end times context. The books of Daniel and Ezekiel are filled with end times prophecy, and the Old Testament is peppered with allusions to the end times.

I'm going to begin with the most important prophetic passage in the Bible. It's the most important because in it, Jesus Himself answers the question about the end.

Let me sketch the setting for you. Jesus and his disciples were leaving the temple grounds in Jerusalem. The disciples were remarking about the buildings around them, and Jesus responded, *"Do you see all these buildings? I tell you the truth, they will be completely demolished. Not one stone will be left on top of another!"*[2]

The group of structures to which Jesus was referring was the grandest architectural feat of that era, and maybe of any era.[3] Which is why, when Jesus predicted the temple's destruction, his followers thought the statement was outrageous. So outrageous, in fact, that they felt compelled to find Him later and ask a question:

> "Later as he was sitting on Mount Olives, his disciples approached and asked him, 'Tell us, when are these things going to happen? What will be the sign of your coming, that the time's up?'
>
> "Jesus said, 'Watch out for doomsday deceivers. Many leaders are going to show up with forged identities, claiming, "I am Christ, the Messiah." They will deceive a lot of people.'"[4]

This has happened already, hasn't it? From Charles Manson

to Muhammad to Bhagwan Shree Rajneesh.

"'When reports come in of wars and rumored wars, keep your head and don't panic. This is routine history; this is no sign of the end. Nation will fight nation and ruler fight ruler, over and over. Famines and earthquakes will occur in various places. This is nothing compared to what is coming.

"'They are going to throw you to the wolves and kill you, everyone hating you because you carry my name. And then, going from bad to worse, it will be dog-eat-dog, everyone at each other's throat, everyone hating each other.

"'In the confusion, lying preachers will come forward and deceive a lot of people. For many others, the overwhelming spread of evil will do them in—nothing left of their love but a mound of ashes.

"'Staying with it—that's what God requires. Stay with it to the end. You won't be sorry, and you'll be saved. All during this time, the good news—the Message of the kingdom—will be preached all over the world, a witness staked out in every country. And then the end will come.'"[5]

This is why I talk about the good news. I have no interest in scaring people. Jesus is good news. He is being talked about all over the world right now. And the devil is in such a panic he is trying to distract and terrorize every Jesus person.

"'But be ready to run for it when you see the monster of desecration set up in the Temple sanctuary. The prophet Daniel described this. If you've read Daniel, you'll know what I'm talking about. If you're living in Judea at the time, run for the hills; if you're working in the yard, don't return to the house to get anything; if you're out in the field, don't go back and get your coat. Pregnant and nursing mothers will have it especially hard.

Hope and pray this won't happen during the winter or on a Sabbath.

"'This is going to be trouble on a scale beyond what the world has ever seen, or will see again. If these days of trouble were left to run their course, nobody would make it. But on account of God's chosen people, the trouble will be cut short.

"'Following those hard times…the Arrival of the Son of Man! It will fill the skies—no one will miss it. Unready people all over the world, outsiders to the splendor and power, will raise a huge lament as they watch the Son of Man blazing out of heaven. At that same moment, he'll dispatch his angels with a trumpet-blast summons, pulling in God's chosen from the four winds, from pole to pole.

"'Take a lesson from the fig tree. From the moment you notice its buds form, the merest hint of green, you know summer's just around the corner. So it is with you: When you see all these things, you'll know he's at the door. Don't take this lightly. I'm not just saying this for some future generation, but for all of you. This age continues until all these things take place. Sky and earth will wear out; my words won't wear out.

"'But the exact day and hour? No one knows that, not even heaven's angels, not even the Son. Only the Father knows.

"'The Arrival of the Son of Man will take place in times like Noah's. Before the great flood everyone was carrying on as usual, having a good time right up to the day Noah boarded the ark. They knew nothing—until the flood hit and swept everything away.

"So stay awake, alert. You have no idea what day your Master will show up. Be vigilant just like that.'"[6]

WHEN: NEAR, BUT NOT CLEAR

When is Jesus coming again? Here's how He answered the question:

> *"...when you see all these things, you can know his return is very near, right at the door. I tell you the truth, this generation will not pass from the scene until all these things take place. ... However, no one knows the day or hour when these things will happen, not even the angels in heaven or the Son himself. Only the Father knows."*[7]

According to Jesus' own words, the day of His next coming is near, but not known. He also said this:

> *"So you, too, must keep watch! For you don't know what day your Lord is coming. ... You also must be ready all the time, for the Son of Man will come when least expected."*[8]

Basically, Jesus said His return could be anytime. This is important. As noted earlier, everything that had to take place before Jesus' return had happened by the time the disciples died.

When I see people preoccupied or obsessed with "signs," I can tell they don't have a true understanding of the end times. We don't need any more signs for Jesus to come. According to my understanding of the Bible, the next thing to happen on the prophetic calendar is Jesus gathering His church from earth and relocating His people to heaven. The temple does not need to be rebuilt first. No additional wars, famines, or natural disasters need to happen first.

In the region where I live, lots of people have been caught up in the predictions that there will be a major earthquake and we'll fall into the sea. We may very well fall into the sea, but that's not the point. We don't need any more earthquakes for the end times to begin in earnest; earthquakes are not critical to the timeline.

People who have a very contemporary view of the end times tend to be unsettled by terrorist leaders or terrorist groups like ISIS. My brother battles Islamic radicalism every day. He's an advocate for the largest group of its kind called Open Doors. At the time of this writing, Open Doors is in more than 60 countries advocating for the rights of people with family members who have been persecuted or killed for their faith in Jesus. [9]

Sadly, what ISIS has done is nothing compared to what Joseph Stalin did to his own people. He starved at least seven million Ukrainians. This kind of madness has been going on for decades, even centuries. Pol Pot, Adolf Hitler, Joseph Stalin, Vladimir Putin, ISIS, Khmer Rouge. It's all part of the timeline.

Jesus' coming is near, but not clear. And it's important to understand that it will never be clear. Some people are fascinated with the Jewish calendar because Jesus' first physical arrival on earth occurred on Passover. The Holy Spirit first introduced His presence on another Jewish holiday: Pentecost. So thousands of scholars and curious people are trying to figure out the significance of "blood moons," what these have to do with Jewish festivals, and what it all may be pointing to and when.

When people try to put a date on Jesus' coming, they are in essence defying what Jesus Himself said. If you think you can guess His arrival date from some lunar calendar, you're betting on a losing horse. The Pharisees couldn't see Him coming the first time, and they knew every detail of every prophecy ever spoken about Him, as well as every significance of every date on the Jewish calendar. Yet some of us think we're going to get a fix on Jesus' arrival by reading a couple of books.

Why did Jesus tell us His return is near, but not tell us when?

Not because He wants us to be afraid. Remember the instruction Jesus gave His disciples? *"Keep your head and don't panic. ... Stay with it to the end. You won't be sorry, and you'll be saved."*[10] God doesn't want you to hear about the end times and go silent. He doesn't want you to ponder what's coming and feel weak and vulnerable. He wants you to get emboldened. As Paul reminds us in his letter to Timothy, *"For God has not given us a spirit of fear and timidity, but of power...."*[11]

Jesus also didn't intend for us to be distracted by dissecting and attempting to interpret every symbolic and figurative reference in Scripture. I honestly don't think we get extra credit for any of that, especially if we're not actively telling others His story and our own story of how He has changed our life.

Jesus told His disciples—and told us through them—that He is coming soon because He wants us be active. He knows us well enough to know that if He told us when "the last minute" will be, we would in all likelihood waste time until then.

If you're a Jesus person, you shouldn't be waiting for the end times; you should be recruiting for the kingdom. You shouldn't be worrying, but witnessing.

WHEN: NOW

The end times began with Jesus' first coming and will end with His second coming. His first arrival was the sign that all of history was moving toward His second. That was 2000 years ago. It may be another five days, five years, or five hundred years before He returns as He promised. And every minute of that time is significant.

Here's one way I like to think of the "when" in which we're living. Have you ever invited people over for dinner, or been a guest for a meal in someone's home? Sometimes, there's a brief period of time when the meal is ready, but the guests have not yet arrived. That's the moment we're living right now. The party is ready and Jesus is eager to begin it, but He is waiting for more guests to accept His invitation.

I don't know when He will come. But I do know this: Every day that passes is somebody's end of the world. And Jesus' desire is that no one would die in this life without knowing Him. It's why He came the first time...

> "For this is how God loved the world: He gave his one and only Son, so that everyone who believes in him will not perish but have eternal life. God sent his Son into the world not to judge the world, but to save the world through him."[12]

...and it's why He's waiting before He returns:

> "But you must not forget this one thing, dear friends: A day is like a thousand years to the Lord, and a thousand years is like a day. The Lord isn't really being slow about his promise, as some people think. No, he is being patient for your sake. He does not want anyone to be destroyed, but wants everyone to repent. But the day of the Lord will come as unexpectedly as a thief."[13]

Just as I have no idea when Jesus will come, I have no idea how long you or I have left to live. But I do know I'm responsible for the time that I'm given here on this earth. I'm responsible for telling the Jesus story to everybody I can. As far as you and I are concerned, the "when" is now. Because it's somebody's end of the world right now.

Maybe you're fascinated with Jesus coming again. You're a dedicated student of Daniel and Ezekiel and Revelation. But your neighbors are on the edge of eternity right now and you're not telling them your Jesus story. You're sitting with your cup of coffee listening to an end times broadcast, or reading an end times book, while your neighbor is headed for hell unless you tell him or her about Jesus.

We don't have to postulate and pontificate about where we are on the prophetic calendar, what the moon looks like, or what Jewish holiday is next. We simply need to know that Jesus is waiting because He loves people, and every day that He waits is an opportunity to invite more people into eternal life with Him.

Friend, as a pastor and someone who has some influence within the body of Christ, I say let's get up and get going. Jesus is coming any minute. Start talking about Him to everyone you know. Please. Our world is poised for His return.

WHERE: THERE

When the end times events described in Scripture begin, they will affect the countries where they physically take place. They will also impact the rest of the world where most of us live, but in vastly different ways.

Because people around the world tend to be nationalistic, many have tried to put their own country in the middle of prophesy as they read through Scripture. Someone once sent me an email posing this question: "Scripture says that in the end times Gog, a great power to the north, is going to come and invade Israel. Is Gog Canada?"

Friend, this was settled before the foundations of the earth. When the Bible says "to the north," it's not talking about to the north of anywhere in the Western world. It's talking about to the north of Israel. The end times are not about America. Or Canada. Or South America. Or England or France or Sweden or Australia. New Jersey isn't in the middle of prophecy. Israel is. It's all about Israel

I mention New Jersey because all of Israel right now is a little bit smaller than New Jersey. You can fit thirty-two Israels in the state of Texas. This little group of people has been under attack, celebrated, and persecuted for all of history. Not because they're powerful. But because they are chosen.[14]

The prophecy from the very beginning has been that the world would continue to battle over this little country. And when end times events begin to unfold, they will be centered around Israel.

> *"On that day I will make Jerusalem an immovable rock. All the nations will gather against it to try to move it, but they will only hurt themselves."*[15]

I once watched a documentary segment on a guy in Texas who claimed to be the antichrist.[16] While I found it entertaining viewing, I'm pretty sure the devil isn't going to come with cowboy boots on. Because Scripture says the end times revolve around Israel—*there*. That place is being fought over. That holy ground, that piece of dirt is going to be contested, as it has been through the ages.

The book of Daniel says there will be an attack from the north.[17] What's north of Israel? Syria. Iraq. Turkey. Russia. The attack will come from these regions. Then someone will rise to power and make peace with Jerusalem and all the parties for seven years. He will rebuild the temple. And three and a half years into the seven-year peace pact, he will say, "Why don't we just declare me the Messiah and I'll call this temple my own?"[18] And then evil will reign for three and a half years.

All of that will happen *there*, in Jerusalem, not in the Western world.

WHERE: HERE

If *there* is Jerusalem. Then *here* is the rest of the world, where I live and you probably do, too.

Will the whole world be touched by end times events? After all, America isn't mentioned in the Scriptures about the end times, and the majority of the world's countries are not mentioned either. I've given this some thought, and I wonder if it is because we will be either not engaged in the conflict or not significantly relevant, or both.

Consider this with me: If every believer in Jesus was suddenly transported from earth to heaven,[19] what would the impact be on your country's armed forces? On government? The postal service? Medical staff? Communications and banking? Whether or not you are a Jesus person yourself, think about how many Jesus people you know. And then think about the sudden impact if every one of them simultaneously left.

Do you understand how pervasive the church of Jesus is? When the World Health Organization talks about how to stop pandemics, they dismiss hospitals entirely and go right to churches. Because if you go to Lesotho, Africa, you'll drive for three hours before you come to one little clinic. You won't see a hospital at all. But you'll see fifty churches. The church is pervasive. It's everywhere.

I believe anywhere there are followers of Jesus, His removal of His church from the earth will have an impact. And the countries with the highest population of Jesus people will be impacted most profoundly.

When will the end times calendar begin in earnest? It's near, but not clear. Which means the time to be preparing and ready is now. Where will the end times happen? They will be centered around Israel. And, as has been the case for centuries, what impacts Israel and God's people will impact the entire world.

WHO

When I look at Scripture's full account of the end times, I see three main characters who play the supporting and lead roles:

- You and me
- The antichrist
- Jesus

YOU & ME

You may not see your name or mine written in the Scriptures about the end times, but there's no question you and I have a key role to play. We are central to the end times.

Think about it in terms of an election in which neither of us is a candidate. Our names aren't on the banners and mailers and lawn signs and advertisements. But why is all of that money spent to produce all of that material, and who is it intended to reach? Us. Because we determine the outcome. Our votes, our support, and our influence all ultimately impact who wins.

I'll admit the end times scenario is different than your average election. For one thing, we already know who wins the contest between the power brokers: Jesus does. What's in play, however, is who wins with Him. Those of us who know Him already are part of His campaign team. And our key role is to recruit anyone and everyone we can to the winners' circle.

The prophet Daniel is a powerful example of what this role looks like:

"I went on praying and confessing my sin and the sin of

my people, pleading with the Lord my God for Jerusalem, his holy mountain. As I was praying, Gabriel, whom I had seen in the earlier vision, came swiftly to me at the time of the evening sacrifice. He explained to me, 'Daniel, I have come here to give you insight and understanding. The moment you began praying, a command was given. And now I am here to tell you what it was, for you are very precious to God. Listen carefully so that you can understand the meaning of your vision.'"[1]

When I read Scripture I try to pay attention to tone as well as data. And it's striking to me that this angel, who came to tell Daniel about things that would happen centuries later, led with, "Daniel, you are very precious to God." So cool. Whatever you're going through right now, you need to process what God is saying to you through His posture toward you: His posture is love. You are important. You and I each have a role, and it's up to us how influential we choose to make it.

> The choices we make, and the actions we take or don't take, make a difference in eternity.

Are you campaigning for the kingdom and for hope and victory? Are you praying like Daniel on behalf of yourself, your people, your city, your country? Or are you spreading fear instead of faith? Are you immobilized by anxiety or apathy, and doing nothing of influence either way? All of these things are consequential. The choices we make, and the actions we take or don't take, make a difference in eternity.

End times prophecy is not theoretical language for us to play around with and debate. It represents actual events on an actual timeline. When the Bible talks about the end times, the antichrist, and the soon return of Jesus, the language is urgent. It uses words like "near," "watch," "ready," "prepared," and "invite." The intent is to compel us to get out into our world and share the love of Jesus as best we can. The Scriptures say I will be held accountable for my mobilization and engagement of you. I want to be found faithful, and I want you to be, too.

In one of Jesus' figurative stories about the end times, he talks about going "out to the street corners and invit[ing] everyone you see" to a great banquet.[2] He's saying, "Go get them now. Invite everybody. The party's about to start." Notice He's not talking about judgment or execution or damnation. There's going to be a party like you've never seen for everyone who's connected to Jesus. And you and I get to hand out the invitations.

If you're a follower of Jesus, there's another role I believe you also play in the end times finale: your absence. I mentioned in the previous chapter that I believe Jesus will collect His bride, the church, from the earth before the major events of the end times begin in earnest.

Jesus told His followers they were salt and light—two metaphors that have applied to every Jesus follower through the ages.[3] Salt is both an enhancer and a preservative. Light penetrates darkness and changes the whole equation. One moment you're stumbling around; then you hit one little switch or strike one little spark, and you can instantly see everything with complete clarity. This is what followers of Jesus are, and the effect we are to have on our world. When we partner with the Holy Spirit to engage and change our community, we shine light into dark corners and preserve the earth so Jesus can rescue more people into His kingdom.

The game of chess has an interesting glossary term: "endgame."

> "An endgame is the very last part of a strategic game.... The last few moves you make...are your endgame. [T]he term...[has] long been used by players to describe what happens when very few pieces are left on the board."[4]

To me, this sounds like what the setting will be when the church has been taken to heaven and only the final players of the end times remain on earth.

When Jesus comes for His people and takes them with Him to heaven, this means salt and light are gone. Things that are being preserved by the church right now—like ideals, principles, morals, and social justice—will begin decaying when the church is no longer here. Things that are now lit and understood will be dark. All of this sets the stage for the antichrist to seize his moment. And what the Bible describes happening under his reign I can't imagine being allowed to take place if the church was still present on earth.

ANTICHRIST

A second character who plays a significant role in the end times is the antichrist.

> "A period of seventy sets of seven has been decreed for your people and your holy city to finish their rebellion, to put an end to their sin, to atone for their guilt, to bring in everlasting righteousness to confirm the prophetic vision, and to anoint the Most Holy Place. Now listen and understand! Seven sets of seven plus sixty-two sets of seven will pass from the time the command is given to rebuild Jerusalem until a ruler—the Anointed One—comes. Jerusalem will be rebuilt with streets and strong defenses, despite the perilous times.
>
> "After this period of sixty-two sets of seven, the Anointed One will be killed, appearing to have accomplished nothing,

and a ruler will arise whose armies will destroy the city and the Temple. The end will come with a flood, and war and its miseries are decreed from that time to the very end. The ruler will make a treaty with the people for a period of one set of seven, but after half this time, he will put an end to the sacrifices and offerings. And as a climax to all his terrible deeds, he will set up a sacrilegious object that causes desecration, until the fate decreed for this defiler is finally poured out on him."[5]

What this passage says, in concert with other accounts in Scripture, is that for seven years the antichrist will be the visually dominant character in the story. He will rebuild in all its splendor the temple in Jerusalem that was destroyed by the Roman Empire. The Jewish people will be living an experience they've dreamed of for centuries.

For three and a half years, the antichrist will make and keep a peace pact with the nations that will elevate him to a place of extreme power and authority. Then he will break that peace by setting up a sacrilegious object in the temple and demanding that people worship him as the Messiah. Three and a half years of hardship and horror will commence before Jesus will put an end to it all and claim the victory He has already won.

I've been asked whether followers of Jesus will recognize the antichrist for who he is. My belief is that Jesus will take His people to heaven before the antichrist makes his rise to power. But if I am wrong about the rapture and the church is still here, I'm inclined to think Jesus people will be able to identify him. Just look at the number of Christians who have been looking for him under every metaphorical rock in every country for centuries.

For generations, fascinated people have been keeping an eye out for and trying to identify the antichrist—attempting to match individuals' positions, credentials, lineage, and actions with the description Scripture gives us. From time to time, a likely candidate is singled out and thoroughly scrutinized. Then he is defeated or dies or retires, and the search begins anew.

Scripture says not only will there be an antichrist, there have already been other antichrists. In our language, "anti" means against. However, the term used in Scripture means not just against Christ but *instead* of Christ. This is someone who presents himself as a deity or savior and demands worship. We have seen several leaders fit this description throughout history, haven't we? Nero, Joseph Stalin, Adolf Hitler, and a few others come to mind.

Here's a thought that is one hundred percent my personal opinion: If you're looking for the antichrist, I recommend keeping an eye on people who are seen as deal brokers. Individuals who seem like they have a broad, nebulous religious system, who don't declare a particular faith and seem to say all truth leads to God. In the overall theological picture, they are compromisers and promoters of compromise.

But do you really want to be flipping through Wikipedia trying to figure out the bio of the antichrist? Or do you want to keep an eye on the spirit that he and others are cultivating? Because if we're not paying attention, we can become numb without even realizing it to the permissive, indiscriminate, passive thinking that will pave the way for someone like the antichrist to rise to prominence.

The identity of the antichrist is not primarily about position. It's about allegiance. It's about what this person will do and the allegiance he will ask for. The antichrist will ask something of you in alignment with the spirit of the age. Here's how he is described in Daniel chapter 11:

> *"The next to come to power will be a despicable man who is*

not in line for royal succession. He will slip in when least expected and take over the kingdom by flattery and intrigue. Before him great armies will be swept away, including a covenant prince. With deceitful promises, he will make various alliances. He will become strong despite having only a handful of followers.

"But he will...reward those who forsake the covenant. ... He will flatter and win over those who have violated the covenant. But the people who know their God will be strong and will resist him.

"Wise leaders will give instruction to many, but these teachers will die by fire and sword, or they will be jailed and robbed. During these persecutions, little help will arrive, and many who join them will not be sincere. And some of the wise will fall victim to persecution. In this way, they will be refined and cleansed and made pure until the time of the end, for the appointed time is still to come.

"The king will do as he pleases, exalting himself and claiming to be greater than every god, even blaspheming the God of gods. ... He will have no respect for the gods of his ancestors...or for any other god, for he will boast that he is greater than them all."[6]

Whoever the antichrist turns out to be, the enemy is already at work preparing a clear pathway for his strategy to succeed. He will ask people to keep swallowing more and more deception. He'll ask them to give a little here, give a little there. He'll ask them to not just love other faiths, but to say that those faiths are equal. Can you see how the culture around us is already working to draw people in this direction?

By the way, do you understand the difference between loving and accepting a Muslim because he is a human being, and saying that the Muslim faith is the same as the Christian faith? I ask the question because I meet people all the time who aren't able to see the difference. Yet the two concepts are wildly different.

If you're a believer, you're called to love everyone even if they defy Christ to your face. If they ask you to go one mile, you go two. We bless those who curse us. It might be the hardest thing you've ever done, but it's what we're called to do. No matter what.

However, loving every person is entirely different from saying all religions are the same. The Bible says only Jesus is the way, the truth, and the life, and the only way to God is through Him.[7] That doesn't leave any room for "equal ground" with other faiths.

Followers of Jesus stand in a position of truth. The good news of Jesus is a matter of fact, not opinion. If you ask three people whether Jesus is the only Son of God, and one says, "Kind of," another says, "No," and the other says, "Yes," there is only one possible conclusion. One person is right and the other two are wrong.

The antichrist will be intent on blurring the lines between yes and no. I see examples every day of how the culture around us is already cultivating this shift. Maybe you see it, too.

Scripture tells us that in the end times, *"Sin will be rampant everywhere, and the love of many will grow cold."*[8] It's not that we will all build a satanic temple or start an after-school Satan club. But maybe we will be more enraptured with our football team than with anything else. Or single-mindedly focused on building our retirement reserves. Or obsessed with escalating our standard of living. Or fixated on finding a spouse.

Watch what happens when we experience economic dip. Almost overnight, the hue and cry becomes, "Give us the guy who can fix this so we can get our boat/vacations/house back."

Money doesn't matter…until it does. And then it's everything. Your hobbies don't matter until they do. And suddenly they're consuming. And you find yourself throwing your faith overboard for some of the most ridiculous things. This is the spirit of the age. This is the spirit in which the antichrist walks, and into which he will be welcomed.

The Bible is crystal clear: the antichrist has a role because Jesus has been diminished and "peace" has been exalted. The antichrist will come from nowhere, perhaps. We may not see him coming. But he'll be able to broker peace and bring excitement and hope in a way that surprises people. He'll deliver more than just hype, and will somehow orchestrate an opus that brings Muslims and Jews together. That'll be something, won't it? He will say to the Jews, "I'm going to give you the temple back." And he will rebuild the temple in all its magnificence, and then he'll move in.

Many people fear the end of the world in terms of technology. They're afraid ISIS will get a dirty bomb and it will all be over. My Bible tells me the world won't end because of technology. The world will end because of theology. The antichrist won't just be trying to get dirty bombs to terrorists. The antichrist will be trying to get you to lay down your passion for Jesus, to walk away from your conviction.

Politics will be a part of the end times. Weapons may be a part. Terrorist groups may be a part. But none of these is central. What's central is you, and the antichrist's work to create compromise and complacency around theology.

JESUS

Given the description of the antichrist's role presented in Scripture, one could easily get the impression that he is the main character of the end times. But he is a significant player for a mere seven years on a timeline of thousands and thousands and thousands of years of history. If this were the Academy Awards, the antichrist wouldn't even be nominated for best supporting actor.

The main character in this story, who eclipses everything and everyone else, is a Nazarene. His name is Jesus. His victory was a sure thing before the conflict ever began.

It doesn't matter who is leading which country, or what country the antichrist comes from. What matters is that Jesus is on the throne. He always has been. He is today. And He always will be.

He died for us. He is pursuing us. He is fighting for us. He is preparing heaven for us. He is coming for us. And He is moving all of history toward the moment when He can begin eternity with us.

WHOLE NEW WORLD

There's a reason the subtitle of this book is "the end times and happily ever after." It's because, like the finale of a TV season or a book in a series, the end of this finale isn't the end. It's got all of the elements of a good finale—battles, allegiances, alliances, crescendo, cliffhanger crises, dramatic pauses, reversals, edge-of-your-seat unknowns. But best of all, it has a sequel. And for people who love Jesus, that next volume is heaven.

> **The ultimate destination, for new beginning and forever, is heaven.**

In fact, it's actually far more accurate to say heaven is the setting for the main story itself. Everything that has happened and will happen before we experience heaven—including the end times—is prelude.

The ultimate destination, the ultimate address for new beginning and forever, is heaven. The lives we are living today are preparing us for life with Jesus in heaven. The relationships we invest in now are the building blocks of relationships we will experience on a whole new level in heaven. The end times are advancing history toward heaven.

So if heaven is such a big deal, and the place Jesus had in mind when He died so we could spend eternity there with Him, what do we know about it? What is it like, why does it matter, and does any of what happens on earth matter there? Will we be like robots who worship God all the time?

As a pastor, I get asked questions like these more frequently than you can imagine.

HEAVEN IS…

It's a point of interest to me that in all of its sixty-six inspired books, a relatively small percentage of Scripture is dedicated to talking about heaven. Here are a few of the most basic facts we are told:

Heaven is where God lives.

> *"The Lord looks down from heaven and sees the whole human race."*[1]

Heaven is where Jesus is today, and where He's coming from when He returns.

> *"When the Lord Jesus had finished talking with them, he was taken up into heaven and sat down in the place of honor at God's right hand."*[2]

> *"Jesus has been taken from you into heaven, but someday he will return from heaven in the same way you saw him go!"*[3]

If we know Jesus, heaven is where we go when we die.

> *"But if I live, I can do more fruitful work for Christ. So I really don't know which is better. I'm torn between two desires: I long to go and be with Christ, which would be far better for me."*[4]

> *"Then he said, 'Jesus, remember me when you come into your Kingdom.' And Jesus replied, 'I assure you, today you will be with me in paradise.'"*[5]

Heaven is the city God is building for us. He is the architect and contractor. For literally thousands of years, God has been preparing His home for you.

> Jesus told His followers, "There is more than enough room in my Father's home. If this were not so, would I have told you that I am going to prepare a place for you? When everything is ready, I will come and get you, so that you will always be with me where I am. And you know the way to where I am going."[6]

> "Abraham was confidently looking forward to a city with eternal foundations, a city designed and built by God."[7]

Heaven is better.

> "But they were looking for a better place, a heavenly homeland. That is why God is not ashamed to be called their God, for he has prepared a city for them."[8]

These are the main facts Scripture gives us about heaven, which are plenty compelling on their own. But the Bible also talks about several nuances of heaven that, to me, are absolutely fascinating to ponder and filled with hope.

HEAVEN IS NEW

Do you like new? I do.

I like new shoes. My son sent me a picture of some shoes the other day and asked, "Dad, you want these?" We have an arrangement. He's cool, he finds what's cool, and he sends it to me.

New is attractive.

Have you ever had a new car, or ridden in someone else's? You may be driving a 1971 Pinto, but you can walk into any mini-mart and buy a "new car smell" air freshener. It's just the smell of new, but if that's all you can afford, you want it.

New is sensory.

Shall we talk new technology? I was at the mall with one of my kids on a day when the Apple Store was introducing a new phone. A couple hundred people were lined up in the mall, just waiting for the doors to open. My phone was pretty new at the time, so I didn't join the line. I kept walking, which happened to be toward the doors of the store. And just as we were walking past those doors, about 30 employees came out. Clearly, their job was to get people excited. They started clapping and cheering and yelling, and pretty soon the couple hundred people were clapping and cheering and yelling. I turned to my child and said, "We're getting a new phone today."

New is exciting!

The first nuance I find interesting about heaven is that God is starting over with everything...except you and me.

"Then I saw a new heaven..."[9]

Can we pause right there for a moment? Sometimes futuristic movies and books depict a new earth. Here, Scripture isn't just talking about a new earth; it's talking about a new heaven! We already noted that heaven is better than earth, right? In eternity, God is creating not just a new earth; He's also doing a new heaven. Because of what the enemy did. The devil is a fallen angel, the Bible tells us. And he didn't fall from Topeka, Kansas; he corrupted the heavens. So God is literally starting over with heaven, to make it one hundred percent new.

"...and a new earth, for the old heaven and the old earth had disappeared. And the sea was also gone."[10]

Have you been in, on, or over the Pacific Ocean? Or the

Atlantic? They are so vast! I've read a couple of books written by author Simon Winchester about the Pacific and the Atlantic, and all the history that has happened in those bodies of water.[11] Yet Scripture tells us God is going to completely redefine all of that.

> "And the one sitting on the throne said, 'Look, I am making everything new!' And then he said to me, 'Write this down, for what I tell you is trustworthy and true.' And he also said, 'It is finished! I am the Alpha and the Omega—the Beginning and the End.'"[12]

Everything new. Except you. Because if you know Him, He already made you new.[13] We read elsewhere in Scripture that our bodies will be new in heaven.[14] But that's not what I'm talking about here. I'm talking about your heart, your spirit. If you believe that when you accept Jesus He gives you a new heart and that's why you go to heaven, then He made you new and started your eternity with Him the minute you said, "Yes."

If you know Jesus, He already made you new the minute you said, "Yes."

Yet the devil tries to hold you back with lies. He says, "You know that thing you did nine years ago, that thing four weeks ago, that thing you got forgiveness for? That's really not forgiven. How could that possibly be forgiven?"

Please hear me on this: Whatever is in your past or your future, it is so forgiven that God is going to wipe out heaven and start over. And you will be there because of what Jesus has done in you already. God is going to start over with the Atlantic, but you are so forgiven right now that you are already new. If you know Jesus, you are so new right now that when Jesus creates a New Jerusalem, you get to live in it with Him.

HEAVEN IS RELATIONAL

Second, the new world is entirely relational. The Bible says that right now, pre-heaven, here on earth, we see things with flawed perspective:

> *"Now we see things imperfectly, like puzzling reflections in a mirror, but then we will see everything with perfect clarity. All that I know now is partial and incomplete, but then I will know everything completely, just as God now knows me completely. Three things will last forever—faith, hope, and love—and the greatest of these is love."*[15]

From where we are now, we aren't able to see the picture God sees, either completely or clearly. So we grope our way through each day, trying to figure stuff out. But all of heaven will be clarity. We will understand. We will be known. People won't just know your name; they will truly know you.

There are a handful of accounts in the New Testament that include people who were either in or from heaven. In one of these narratives, three disciples were praying with Jesus when two long-deceased prophets suddenly appeared. We know Peter knew exactly who these men were because he referred to them by name.[16] How did he know them? I'm pretty sure they weren't wearing nametags that said, "Hello, my name is Elijah." Instead, I believe he recognized Moses and Elijah because they were still Moses and Elijah. In heaven you'll be you, but you'll be understood and known completely for who you are.

Everything about the earth, including who we are and how we are seen and known by others, is tainted by sin. God sees me as completely forgiven today only because He sees me through the purifying "filter" of Jesus' blood. He is also growing me to be, and showing me more every day, who He created and destined me to be. But I promise you: I can't trust you right now with who I really

I am, and you probably can't trust me with who you are.

In contrast, in the new world, where all is known and all is forgiven, nobody will be covering up who they really are. We will know each other and be known completely. There will be no guilt, no shame, no tears, no pain.

Most importantly, we will live in relationship with God in a way we never have here on earth:

> "I heard a loud shout from the throne, saying, 'Look, God's home is now among his people! He will live with them, and they will be his people. God himself will be with them. He will wipe every tear from their eyes, and there will be no more death or sorrow or crying or pain. All these things are gone forever. ... To all who are thirsty I will give freely from the springs of the water of life. All who are victorious will inherit all these blessings, and I will be their God, and they will be my children.'"[17]

I have spent a lot of time imagining what it will be like to live not only in relationship with God, but in community with Him. I know He is with me all the time already. In fact, I talk with Him almost constantly about nearly everything. But this verse implies His presence will be different in heaven than we experience it now, and relational on a whole new level. I can't even tell you how eager I am for this new life with God. And I believe it's what He has longed for and orchestrated all of history toward, ever since *"In the beginning."*

HEAVEN IS SENSORY

Third, the new world is entirely sensory. Not a single feature of it that is described to us in Scripture comes even close to being dull. Have you read John's description of heaven in Revelation chapter 21?

> "Then I saw a new heaven and a new earth, for the old heaven and the old earth had disappeared. And the sea was also gone. And I saw the holy city, the new Jerusalem, coming down from God out of heaven like a bride beautifully dressed for her husband. ...
>
> "It shone with the glory of God and sparkled like a precious stone—like jasper as clear as crystal. The city wall was broad and high, with twelve gates guarded by twelve angels. And the names of the twelve tribes of Israel were written on the gates. There were three gates on each side—east, north, south, and west. The wall of the city had twelve foundation stones, and on them were written the names of the twelve apostles of the Lamb.
>
> "The wall was made of jasper, and the city was pure gold, as clear as glass. The wall of the city was built on foundation stones inlaid with twelve precious stones: the first was jasper, the second sapphire, the third agate, the fourth emerald, the fifth onyx, the sixth carnelian, the seventh chrysolite, the eighth beryl, the ninth topaz, the tenth chrysoprase, the eleventh jacinth, the twelfth amethyst.
>
> "The twelve gates were made of pearls—each gate from a single pearl! And the main street was pure gold, as clear as glass.
>
> "I saw no temple in the city, for the Lord God Almighty and the Lamb are its temple. And the city has no need of sun or moon, for the glory of God illuminates the city, and the Lamb is its light. The nations will walk in its light, and the kings of the world will enter the city in all their glory. Its gates will never be closed at the end of day because there is no night there. And all the nations will bring their glory and honor into the city."[18]

As you read these sentences, don't think just in functional pictures. The writer is trying to describe a dream to you, a vision he was given and told to write down for us. This is prose, written to let you know you are going to be part of a sensory experience in heaven like you've never encountered.

Gold has texture, beauty, and value. It is among the materials we consider precious on earth. Yet here we read that gold—so pure it is as clear as glass—is used as pavement in heaven. And sapphires, emeralds, and pearls are mere building materials.

> **In God's economy, we are works of art.**

When I became a Jesus person I was just a little guy. One weekend the pastor at our church mentioned streets of gold, and I remember either asking my dad a question or making a comment about that idea as we drove home after church. Whatever it was that I asked or said, I clearly remember my dad correcting me. He said, "Son, the Bible doesn't mention streets of gold because gold is super valuable in heaven. The point is that what's valuable here means nothing there."

Think about how cool that is. We barter days of our lives here for a little band of gold with a few diamonds. We labor to obtain things that are already decaying. Yet heaven is so fabulous that the stuff we value so highly right now is building materials and surface covering there. We walk on it.

Now think the thought that, in the middle of all this, is you. The King is the centerpiece of heaven, but He never intended to be there alone. He created heaven for you. In God's economy, we are works of art. Streets of gold are nothing compared to you. You are more important and valued than amethyst, chrysolite, and topaz. You are a royal resident because you honor the King.

Doesn't that make you think differently about what you're

investing your life in today?

I also love the picture this passage gives us of the radiance of Jesus. Jesus shines. I don't think this reference is just a metaphor. I really believe heaven will have no sun and no moon because Jesus will be so present with us and His glory so luminous that every other light source will be redundant.

Perhaps I believe this so strongly because I've seen glimpses of this here on earth. I shared dinner one evening with three Muslim friends who have all found Jesus. For an hour and forty-five minutes we just talked about Jesus, and Jesus was literally shining through these people.

On another occasion, a friend was telling me about how he had shared Jesus with some colleagues. An opportunity had emerged and the topic of Jesus had come up. I was on the edge of my seat waiting to hear what happened next. What happened was that one of my friend's associates turned to him and said, "Wow. Look at your face. You're like, glowing!"

This is why Jesus is my obsession. I don't think church can do that for you. I don't think a denomination or religion can do what I'm talking about. If you know Jesus, love Jesus, know you're forgiven by Jesus, and know you're not carrying guilt and shame... somehow, He leaks out.

And heaven will be that times a million, times hundreds and hundreds of millions. No wonder there's no sun or moon. There's Him. Can you even imagine?

If I invite you to my house, I try to clean up. I light candles. I put on music. I want it to smell good. I want it to look good. I want the cushions soft, the food savory. Because I love you. And God is doing the same for us in heaven. Because He loves us.

Scripture tells us heaven will be an extremely sensory place—of color and sound, texture and light, honor and glory. And God created you with senses and the ability to experience all of it. Because He loves you.

HEAVEN IS A REWARD

If our destination is heaven, where we will get to be with God and He wants us there, why do we first have to do life on earth?

This question has been framed with different words in countless ways. Every time it comes down to this idea: God, how come You don't just give me what You're asking me to discover?

> God wants you to discover who He is, so He can show you who He created you to be.

Worded that starkly, it seems audacious, doesn't it? After all, we are creation and He is Creator. Then again, I've been known to ask an audacious question from time to time. Maybe you have, too. So let's answer it.

God is simultaneously artist, engineer, and architect. He designed and created a perfect system within which He gives us the opportunity to choose our eternity. He asks us to discover Him and choose Him, and in the process He shows us who He created us to be. It's really quite beautiful.

God isn't toying with us or playing hard to get. He wants to be chosen. In fact, He stacks the deck in His favor because He essentially designed us to be drawn to Him. And He has been giving the same invitation, the same choice to accept or reject, since long before He sent His own Son. Look at this passage from

Deuteronomy, the fifth book in the Old Testament.

> "This command I am giving you today is not too difficult for you, and it is not beyond your reach. It is not kept in heaven, so distant that you must ask, 'Who will go up to heaven and bring it down so we can hear it and obey?' It is not kept beyond the sea, so far away that you must ask, 'Who will cross the sea to bring it to us so we can hear it and obey?' No, the message is very close at hand; it is on your lips and in your heart so that you can obey it.

> "...I have given you the choice between life and death, between blessings and curses. Now I call on heaven and earth to witness the choice you make. Oh, that you would choose life, so that you...might live! You can make this choice by loving the Lord your God, obeying him, and committing yourself firmly to him. This is the key to your life."[19]

God wants you to discover who He is, so He can show you who He created you to be. Every step you take in His direction unlocks wisdom and insight.[20] When you pursue Jesus and honor Jesus, you discover more and more of just how sweet He is, and how He created you to be.

This is a great, adventuresome life. And heaven is a reward, not an entitlement. God is never going to set up a system where you get an entitlement. Grace: yes. Blessing: yes. Forgiveness: yes. Love: more than you can fathom. Inheritance: beyond your imagination. Entitlement: no.

Heaven is a gift from Him. We can choose to reject it. Or we can choose to receive it, unwrap it, and enjoy it.

HEAVEN IS YOUR HOME

Finally, heaven is home. Heaven is not a hotel. It's not a

resort. It's your heritage. It is your home.

Paul writes in Philippians, *"But we are citizens of heaven, where the Lord Jesus Christ lives. And we are eagerly waiting for him to return as our Savior."*[21]

> The point of absolutely everything is this: we're not perfect, Jesus is, and we need His forgiveness.

You obviously don't live there at the moment, but if you know Jesus, you are already a citizen. You already have a passport. You don't need a visa or a green card. You simply have to walk in the door and you will be more welcome and at home in heaven than you have ever been on earth.

I'll be the first to admit: I know very little about heaven. These pages are pretty much the sum total of what I've found in Scripture, with some of my own conjecture and imaginings thrown in. But I know how to get there. And I know why I want to get there.

Jesus.

Jesus is the way, the truth, and the life. He's the way to heaven.[22] And He's the reason to be there. The more I know Jesus, the more I look forward to being with Him in heaven.

Would you like to receive the forgiveness of Jesus and become new? The point of absolutely everything is this: we're not perfect, He is, and we need His forgiveness. This is why my obsession is Jesus. He makes it so easy. We just have to say yes.

WHAT NOW?

I read stacks of books. I subscribe and listen to a curated selection of podcasts. Much of the television I watch is on the History channel and PBS.[1] In other words, I plow through a ton of material.[2]

And whenever I close the cover on the final page of a book, sign out of a podcast, or turn off the TV, I try to take at least a few moments to ponder what I've read, heard, or seen. Were there any interesting ideas? Was there some unique perspective? What should I do with them?

The operative word here is "do."

A finale, by definition, is meant to move you. To feel something. Think something. Maybe even do something.

At a minimum, I encourage you to give further thought to what you've read here. Talk to Jesus and the Holy Spirit. Ask them your questions and really listen for the answers.

A finale, by definition, is meant to move you.

And then, I hope you'll do even more than that. If I said to you, "This is the Super Bowl and we are starting the fourth quarter," I doubt you'd respond with, "Hey, this has been great, but I've got some other stuff I gotta go do." I think you'd say, "Okay! Let's finish this thing!"

At the risk of sounding like every generation that has come before my own, I think we're in the fourth quarter of the biggest "game" of all time. And I want to be watchful and prepared for

Jesus' return, as the Scripture tells us to do. Whether He comes during my lifetime or my grandchildren's or their grandchildren's, I have nothing to lose and everything to gain by living as if it may happen tomorrow.

Here are a few ways I'm working at doing that. I would love it if you would consider joining me.

STUDY SCRIPTURE

I think it bears repeating that the Bible talks about the end times differently than it talks about any other topic. It promises blessing to those who study end times prophecy and obey its instructions. It urges awareness and understanding. It promises reward to those who are prepared and ready when Jesus returns.[3]

I know how people feel about the end times. There's worry and fear and doubt.

In relation to this topic, someone once asked me, "How do I learn to doubt my doubts?" Great question. Our doubts expose our own ignorance, not God's insufficiency. When we have doubt, it simply means we don't know enough yet.

If you really want to quash your doubts, I encourage you to throw yourself into studying the Bible—all of it. Look at what Scripture says about why we should study it, and what happens when we do:

> *"All Scripture is inspired by God and is useful to teach us what is true.... God uses it to prepare and equip his people to do every good work."*[4]

> *"[I]f someone asks about your hope as a believer, always be ready to explain it."*[5]

> *"Work hard so God can say to you, 'Well done.' ... Know*

what his Word says and means."[6]

My paraphrase: study so you can please God, so you can have confidence in you, and so you are ready for anything.

I've been a student of Jesus and the Bible for a few decades now. I confess I stayed away from studying the end times for many of those years. The book of Revelation was intimidating to me. The book of Daniel was confusing. I took an entire class on the book of Daniel, and was more stymied at the end of the course than I had been at the beginning.

But some years ago, I decided: If there's a blessing in that book, I'm going to read Revelation and I'm going to study and I'm going to study and I'm going to study.

Without question, it has been a worthwhile pursuit. Do I know everything there is to know about the end times? Am I done studying? Not even close. If you ask me about much of the specific symbolism Scripture uses to describe this coming season on God's timeline, my answer is still, "I don't know."

Don't let the enemy scare you away from a blessing God wants you to have.

But I can tell you that learning more about the end times has brought greater nuance and insight to my view of Scripture and the scope of God's plan. It has deepened my understanding of God's heart and the Holy Spirit's work. And it has enriched my relationship with Jesus. My faith is stronger and my hope is greater than ever before.

In addition, it has been an absolute blessing to be able to use what God has taught me to encourage others and help them understand. To give peace where there has been anxiety. To extend excitement where there has been fear. To offer courage and purpose where there has been panic and paralysis.

Perhaps you're like I was: intimidated by the topic, but interested in the blessing. Don't let the enemy scare you away from a blessing God wants you to have. Know what the Bible says about the end times—the events and key players, and what we're instructed to do with this knowledge.

If you're willing to be a student of the end times, here's where I recommend starting:

- Read all of the book of Revelation.
- Read Daniel 7-12.
- Read Ezekiel 37-39.
- Read Matthew 24.
- Read Mark 13.
- Read 2 Thessalonians 2.

And then, frankly, read the rest of the Bible. You may be surprised by how much of Scripture addresses the end times, from Old Testament prophecy to Jesus' parables and Paul's letters to the churches in the New Testament.

I also recommend you read Scripture first, and commentaries second. Trust the Holy Spirit to be the good commentator He is. If you're a Jesus person, the Holy Spirit will help you understand. In fact, Jesus called the Holy Spirit *"the Spirit of truth,"* and promised that He would *"guide you into all truth"* and *"tell you about the future."*[7]

In recent years, I've found myself becoming ambivalent toward "study Bibles." I especially don't recommend them to new followers of Jesus approaching the Bible for the first time. Because here's what happens: You read John 3:16. And then you read the small print at the bottom of the page that says what some scholar from Tuscaloosa said *about* John 3:16 as if it were *equal value*.

Study notes are not of equal value to John 3:16. Read the Scripture, let the Holy Spirit work on you a little bit, and if it really presents a conundrum for you, then get out a commentary or consult someone you know is a follower of Jesus and a student of Scripture.

With that premise in mind, there are more than a few resources I've found extremely helpful in my own study of the end times. Some of my favorites are:

- Greg Laurie's *"Book of Revelation"* webcast series[8]
- Joel C. Rosenberg's blog[9]
- *Christianity 101* by Gilbert Bilezikian[10]
- *The Rapture* and *The Final Antichrist,* both by Don Stewart[11]
- *Jon Courson's Application Commentary: New Testament* by Jon Courson[12]
- *Letters from a Skeptic: A Son Wrestles with His Father's Questions about Christianity* by Greg and Edward Boyd[13]

SHARE YOUR STORY

Equally as important as study is talking about this stuff. Nothing helps you see all sides of an idea like talking about it with someone else. And if you're a follower of Jesus, nothing strengthens your faith like sharing your faith. Many Jesus people lose their fervor for Jesus because all they've ever cared about is whether or not they're going to heaven. They never invite anybody to meet Jesus, come to church, come to their house, or even meet for coffee. They never tell their Jesus story.

If you're not sharing your story, you may be forgetting your story. It's my conviction that someone who believes and follows Jesus is also someone who talks about what Jesus is doing and is part of the action. I'm not just watching what's happening. *I am* what's happening. *You are* what's happening. Tell your Jesus story. Ask others to tell you theirs. And if they don't have a Jesus story yet, ask if they would like to have one and tell them how they can.

SEE THE SIGNS

Jesus gave His disciples a detailed yet cryptic description of events that would happen near the time of His return. And then He told them to *"keep watch"* and *"be ready."*[14]

Remember when we talked about how study of the end times requires wisdom? This is one of those areas that gets out of hand unless wisdom and Scripture are kept firmly *in* hand.

Part of the end times mania/fascination—books, programs, etc.—is that people are continually grabbing headlines and trying to jam them into the Bible. I understand how and why people get spun into a froth in a twenty-four-hour news cycle. But we have to learn to think a different way—not in the moment, but over the ages.

For example, when the prophet Daniel was shown the prophecy he recorded for us, he was asked to put the contemporary aside and instead view it through a telescopic lens that extended long beyond his lifetime. Do you know where Daniel was living? In Iran. Iran is actually part of the immediate setting of the end times story. And the head of the Persian Empire in Daniel's day could easily have been viewed as the antichrist the prophecy describes.

If anybody had the opportunity to get worked up about the political situation of the day in relation to end times prophecy, it was the Jesus people living in Rome or Daniel living in Persia. Yet what we see modeled in their lives is fervent dedication to God, and a sense of urgency about communicating His truth to those around them.

My encouragement to you is this: Watch what's going on in our world through the lens of the signs Jesus told us to watch for. Stay tethered to the anchor of Scripture. Continuously talk and listen to Jesus and the Holy Spirit for the perspective and guidance they alone can provide.

With all of these as my filter, there are two main things I pay attention to as I wake up each day and engage with the world: alliances and allegiances.

Alliances

An alliance is a union or association formed for mutual benefit, especially between countries or organizations.[15]

In our world right now there's an alliance called the European Union—often referred to as the EU. This coalition took some decades to come together, but in the most recent generation has become a significant force. It is a monetary alliance. Meaning, its members don't have the same policies. The EU doesn't have one army. It doesn't have one prime minister.

For a long time, prophesy-minded people have been paying attention to the EU because the Bible talks about ten nations coming together to attack Israel in the end times. And it generally tells us they will be located in Eastern Europe and the Middle East. We don't know which countries these will be specifically, and the Bible doesn't pinpoint for us what will bring them together.[16]

Clearly, some significant shifting and regrouping will have to take place to facilitate the formation of this ten-nation coalition. But when I see, for instance, an anchor country like Britain vote to leave the European Union, I wonder if some of that shifting is beginning. I start watching to see what Germany will do now. And Turkey.

The other thing I do with respect to alliances is pray.

The Bible says, *"Pray for the peace of Jerusalem,"*[17] so I pray for the peace of Jerusalem. I'm no foreign relations expert, but I know what the Bible says about Israel being a special place for a special people. And because Jerusalem is close to God's heart, it's important to me and to you.

Lastly, I pray for God's kingdom to come soon, and for His will to be done on earth as it is in heaven.[18]

Allegiances

Allegiance is loyalty or commitment to a superior or to a group or cause.[19]

In recent years the most common forms of conflict, attack, and terror we've seen throughout the world have been bombing and killing—by various people and groups for various named reasons. At first glance, these may seem divergent and unrelated to each other. But to some extent, I think more of them than not can be viewed as individual strikes in an overall battle for people's allegiance.

People acting out of misguided allegiance are targeting other people based on religious beliefs, lifestyle choices, race, politics, and more. I even think the widely pervasive bullying we see in our schools and throughout social media is an example of this as well.

But here's something I also believe because I've seen it firsthand—over and over again, in my own hometown and around the world from Washington D.C. to Afghanistan and India and Tibet: Despite what our newsfeeds and headlines may tell us, people around the world are crying out for the Messiah.

The biggest revival in the world right now is in Iran. They cannot keep Bibles coming into the country fast enough. It's crazy. They outlawed the New Testament, and nothing is hotter than the New Testament right now in Iran.

People in the east (China, Korea, Tibet) are all talking about the Back to Jerusalem movement. Have you heard of it? Google it. It's exciting stuff. The overall premise is that the gospel started in Jerusalem and primarily spread west on its advance *"into all the world."*[20] Now it has circled the globe and is making its way back to Jerusalem, in particular through an influx of Chinese missionaries who have taken up the charge of delivering the gospel message to the Middle Eastern population living between China's east coast and Jerusalem.

Israel has never had a significant revival. But I believe one is on the horizon.

What about the escalating oppression we've seen by Islamic extremists? In my opinion, I think we are watching the end of the Muslim world. The word that comes to mind when I think of the current state of the Muslim faith is *distress*—a state of danger or desperate need.[21]

I think anytime people are strapping bombs to their best and brightest, that's not a sign they're winning the war. It's a sign of desperation. Remember World War II, when Japan was sending its pilots on kamikaze bombing missions? The underlying message was: "We're desperate. We're not winning."

When we read Ezekiel's account of end times prophecy, we don't find a description of para-national organizations. He's not talking about ISIS. He's talking about nations.

Currently, a huge chunk of Russia is Muslim. The birthrate among Protestant and Orthodox people in the former Soviet states is in a nosedive, while the birthrate among Muslims is climbing steeply. If the current trend continues, Russia will be a Muslim country in three decades. France is on track to become a Muslim country.

At the same time, we see them killing each other, themselves, and their children in the name of their allegiance. I plan to pay attention to what happens when the Muslim religion goes into full arrest and an entire group of nations is searching for something or someone to tether to. It's just my own supposal, but to me, this seems like a perfect opportunity for an antichrist to step in with a solution everyone is seeking.

Which is when allegiance will matter most of all.

When you hear people talk about the antichrist, the mark of the beast, etc., the conversation, at its heart, is about allegiance. Who do you confess as Lord and Savior? Nobody will get the mark of the beast accidentally. No one will be saying, "Hey, I got this number and I don't know what it means." Because it will be very clear that it is a confession of your heart.

All of this study and talk and speculating about signs

and symbols is interesting. But if we're not careful, it can be a distraction from what's really important. The real capital at stake here is not territories. It's not caliphates. It's your allegiance.

It comes down to the question Jesus asked His disciples: *"Who do you say I am?"*[22]

Our confession matters. Jesus described allegiance to Him like this:

> *"If any of you wants to be my follower, you must give up your own way, take up your cross daily, and follow me. If you try to hang on to your life, you will lose it. But if you give up your life for my sake, you will save it. And what do you benefit if you gain the whole world but are yourself lost or destroyed? If anyone is ashamed of me and my message, the Son of Man will be ashamed of that person when he returns in his glory and in the glory of the Father and the holy angels."*[23]

Are you willing to be more identified with Jesus than you are with Christianity? Do you understand the difference between the two?

The conversation, at its heart, is about allegiance.

Christianity is a system Jesus never talked about. Ever. It's not an altogether bad system, but when the system pushes out the central character, you've lost the point. We see this illustrated throughout the Bible, from the nation of Israel to the Jewish leaders in Jesus' day, to the earliest churches of believers. And we have continued to see it in the denominations that shaped the heritage of the churches we attend today.

Allegiance to a church or a family tradition or a book or a music style is not allegiance to Jesus.

None of the disciples was a member of a denomination. They didn't have a Bible. They didn't carry around New Testaments. They didn't do devotions. They didn't grow up going to Awana.[24] They never went to Promise Keepers.[25] Never attended a denominational meeting. None of it. And yet I am one hundred percent positive every one of them is in heaven. Why? They knew Jesus.

When I decide and you decide, "I'm going to get up every morning and I'm going to talk about Jesus and talk to Jesus and think about Jesus and say the name of Jesus and think about what Jesus would want me to do," this is what keeps Jesus central. This is why every church and every follower of Jesus must remain focused on Him—loving everybody, accepting everybody, welcoming everybody, and telling them about Jesus.

If this really is the fourth quarter, and alliances and allegiances are shifting toward alignment with the final game clock countdown, it's time for each of us to check our own allegiance, and then lovingly do our part to help others align their allegiance as well. Scripture says the Holy Spirit is convicting *"the world of its sin, and of God's righteousness, and of the coming judgment,"* and that the *"fields are already ripe for harvest."*[26] If we just open our mouths and talk about Jesus, we're going to start reaping what the Holy Spirit has already been cultivating.

Q & A

As I've mentioned earlier, my desire with these few words is not to tell you what to think, but to inspire you to think, and teach you how to think.

The questions below are a mere handful of hundreds people have asked me as a pastor. If you've studied any of these yourself, you know answers and opinions vary widely. Significantly different points of view are held by good people who love Jesus and have studied their Bibles with an earnest desire to discern truth.

The answers I give here are my opinions, based on my study of Scripture and relationship with Jesus. Let's not fight about them. I'm giving you the answers I think I understand. And if your thoughtful study of Scripture and leading by the Holy Spirit leads you to a different answer, let's be okay with that. As a friend of mine says, "It's not worth breaking fellowship over." Let's simply appreciate that we're both following Jesus' instruction to pay close attention so we receive even more understanding.[1]

What do pre-tribulation, mid-tribulation, and post-tribulation mean? And when do you believe Jesus is coming with regard to these?

These terms refer to the timeline of a seven-year pact the antichrist will make with Israel. This entire seven-year period is referred to as the tribulation. Pre-tribulation refers to the time period before the pact begins. Mid-tribulation refers to a time period three and a half years into this pact, when the antichrist will declare himself God, claim the temple as his own, and begin a reign of terror. Post-tribulation refers to the end of it all, when the antichrist has been defeated by Jesus Himself.

At what point on this timeline will Jesus come for His people? I believe the Bible indicates certain things cannot happen in the end times with Jesus people present.[2] So I believe the church will be gathered to heaven before the tribulation.

How does the Feast of Trumpets factor in?

The Bible isn't clear about it and Jesus didn't talk about it. This is my answer to everything having to do with the Jewish calendar. Even though Jesus spoke about the end times in significant detail, He never said a word about the Jewish calendar. It could be significant; I'm not saying it's not. After all, it was significant in His first arrival. But I don't know anything about the connection, or lack thereof, between the Jewish festivals the end times. And neither do you.

But I do know this: The Bible's not trying to scare us; it's trying to save us. If there is something essential for us to know, God wants us to know it. Let's make this thing about Jesus. You can have so much more joy and peace when you focus on Jesus.

As the end draws near, do we fight it? Or do we pursue the events that will lead to the end? Do we attempt to fight the plan, as Peter did when he cut off the guard's ear, or do we let it play out silently?

This is a profound question. If you're a leader, you deal with it on some level much of the time.

One biography I read about Ronald Reagan mentioned that this was one of his great dilemmas. He was a man who believed in the end times.[3] I may be overstating it, but he apparently wrestled with the idea of his own responsibility or influence with regard to these events and their timing. Isn't that fascinating? To know what you know about the end times, and then be put in a position where you're negotiating with Iran?

Currently in our State Department, many if not most of the people in positions of negotiation are atheists. I know this because of a trip I took to Zurich to meet with sixteen Iranian ayatollahs. At this meeting, I shared my testimony of how I met Jesus. For an hour afterward, these ayatollahs asked me questions. About Jesus. When things finally wrapped up, a former ambassador approached me and said something like, "That was amazing. I've never seen anything like it. The State Department needs to hear that."

I asked, "Oh really? Tell me about that." And he said, "Our State Department has been trained under this premise: all of our enemies will be atheists." Because for fifty years our major enemy was the Soviet Union. So everyone who went to college and trained to be a diplomat during that era was trained, "Don't talk about God. Don't talk about God." And then, overnight, all of our enemies are radical theists.

So now we have people who sit at the Iranian desk in the State Department, who don't speak the language and don't believe in God, trying to negotiate with people who do. Meanwhile, the Iranians would rather talk to an infidel like me than to an atheist. Because although they think I'm in error, they think an atheist is a fool.

Back to the question. I think the answer is that you just share Jesus because there's no way you can restrain Him. Even a man in the most influential position on earth still isn't powerful enough to roll back God's plan. So I think you just share your faith and you're faithful. After all, what else can we do? You may work for a newspaper, work at a restaurant, be a student, be raising kids. Wherever we are, we can share Jesus. Everybody reading this has something to do with the end times. Jesus is waiting so more will be saved. If you're eager for His return, start taking people out to coffee and telling them why you have the hope you have.

What will happen to the beloved pets of the people taken to heaven when the rapture occurs?

Did you know the Bible says the godly care for their animals?[4] And that God cares for both people and animals?[5] God is more interested in your pets than you are. They're His creation, not your creation. I don't know what happens to specific pets, but I do know heaven will be full of His creation. The Bible says the wolf will dwell with the lamb, for instance.[6] I don't think that's just a metaphor. I think all of His creation will be at peace with each other and not at war with each other. When you see a wolf savaging a lamb for survival today, you're looking at part of the fall of man in the Garden of Eden. You're looking at what was not meant to be. The Bible says there will be a new heaven and a new earth. We'll have new bodies. Maybe your pets will have new bodies, too. I don't know. But I know God loves you and He loves His creation, including your kitty cat.

In 2 Thessalonians 2:11, what does the phrase, "God will" mean? What is God's role?

This is a question that comes up in the Old Testament, as well. The same language is used in the account of the Jews' escape from Egypt. Scripture says God hardened the heart of Pharaoh.[7] The question is, essentially, at what point does God expedite the storyline by giving people over to their consequences?

I read it like this: This statement in 2 Thessalonians 2:11 is similar to the statement in Romans 1 that says, "God gave them over in the sinful desires of their hearts."[8] It's saying that in those times, people will believe the antichrist first, follow him second, and crave him third. And God will eventually say, "Have it your way. I'm not going to restrain you anymore."

How do I know I'm a good enough Jesus person that I will go to heaven?

You're not! You misunderstand the notion of grace. You're not good enough, so you receive Jesus. And by doing so, you're getting in on His goodness, not yours. I like this question because it reflects what so many people think. We accept Jesus, live for Jesus, and love Jesus. Yet we're uneasy about our everyday lives and downright scared about His return. Why? Because the enemy wants to steal our joy. We don't get accepted by God because we are virtuous. What makes us think we will get an upgrade because we're virtuous? I'm going to heaven in the rapture because I'm with Jesus.

Do you believe in predestination?

Predestination is a view that God has already decided who gets saved and who doesn't get saved. That's a very quick paraphrase of the concept. I'm leery of "isms" in general. Jesus walked the earth as a man two thousand years ago. John Calvin lived five hundred years ago. So the church was thriving for fifteen hundred years just fine without Calvinism, without predestination. The same is true of the opposite opinion, which is called Arminianism. Isms can be dangerous.

Here's what I see in Scripture: God is a partner in our salvation in ways we don't understand. And at the same time, each of us has a choice. So I believe your will is significant. Not because you're a god, but because God Himself allows you to be a partner in your own rescue. Where that begins and He ends, or where He stops Himself and you begin, I don't know. But I believe people get to choose to go to heaven, and that your decision matters in an eternal way.

I know we strive for peace, but couldn't we be fooled by the enemy in the pursuit of peace?

You don't want to make peace over moral issues. But you do want to make peace over security issues. Our Muslim friends believe Jesus is a prophet. And we believe Jesus is the Son of God. We make peace not by compromising our doctrine, but by compromising and negotiating how we can agree to disagree. I believe in making peace, but not by compromising the truth.

Jesus taught about hell as well as heaven. Why are churches today less and less about hell?

We live in a dispensation of grace, where there is still time for people to say yes to Jesus. And with my dying breath, I will not condemn people. I will call them to the light instead of cursing the darkness. The power of life and death is in the tongue. And I'm convinced that talking about what will happen if you do something is far more compelling than talking about what will happen if you don't.

That's why I talk about Jesus. Jesus. Jesus. Because the winsomeness of Jesus is far more captivating than the fear of hell. In my experience, the fear of hell lasts very briefly. In contrast, Jesus has been called the Hound of Heaven.[9] I love that picture. Jesus is after you in the most loving way, trying to woo you and win you. That's the example I'm choosing to follow, whether we're talking about the end times or any other topic you can name.

Jesus.

NOTES

[1] Finale." *Merriam-Webster.com.* Merriam-Webster, n.d. Apr. 2017.

PROLOGUE

[1] "Choose Your Own Adventure is a series of children's gamebooks where each story is written from a second-person point of view, with the reader assuming the role of the protagonist and making choices that determine the main character's actions and the plot's outcome." Wikipedia contributors. "Choose Your Own Adventure." Wikipedia, The Free Encyclopedia. Wikipedia, The Free Encyclopedia, 9 Apr. 2018. Web. 26 Jun. 2018.

WHAT NOT TO THINK

[1] You may be more familiar with the term, "Christian." But because Jesus never talked about "Christians" or "Christianity," I call people who love and follow Jesus simply, "Jesus people."

[2] Lindsey, Hal. *The Late Great Planet Earth.* Grand Rapids: Zondervan, 1970.

[3] Whisenant, Edgar C. *88 Reasons Why the Rapture Will Be in 1988.* Whisenant/World Bible Society, 1988.

[4] Customer Review contributors. *"88 Reasons Why the Rapture Will Be in 1988."* Amazon.com. Web. Feb. 1, 2009.

WHY

[1] Revelation 1:3
[2] Luke 12:35-37
[3] Luke 12:37b

85

4 Luke 12:38

5 Luke 12:38-41

6 Luke 12:42-45a

7 Luke 12:45-47

8 Luke 12:48

9 I address this in greater detail in later chapters, but my basic belief is that the church, the comprehensive group of people who believe in Jesus, is the restraining force referred to in 1 Thessalonians 4:16-17 and 2 Thessalonians 2:6-7; and that the church will be removed from the earth and taken to heaven before all or most events described as the "great tribulation" occur (Daniel 12:1; Revelation 3:10; Matthew 24:30-31; Mark 13:26-27; 1 Corinthians 15:51-52). The time of "great tribulation" is the period of seven years described in the Bible during which the antichrist will rise to power and rule (Daniel 9:27; Matthew 24:21; Revelation 7:14, 13:5).

10 2 Peter 3:3-5a

11 2 Peter 3:5b-9

12 Mark 16:19; Ephesians 1:19-22; Hebrews 1:3

13 Genesis 3:1-5

14 Isaiah 14:12-14; Ezekiel 28:12-18

15 Matthew 24:15-16; Mark 13:14

WEIRD + WISDOM

1 "Weird." *Dictionary.com Unabridged.* Random House, Inc. Apr. 2017.

2 "Metaphysical." *Merriam-Webster.com.* Merriam-Webster, n.d. Web. Apr. 2017

3 Revelation 13:16-18, emphasis mine

WHEN & WHERE

[1] Mecklin, John, editor. Science and Security Board. *2017 Doomsday Clock Statement.* thebulletin.org/clock/2017. Bulletin of the Atomic Scientists, Feb. 2017.

[2] Matthew 24:1-2

[3] Although it was torn down in 70 A.D., we know the temple's description because its design and construction is meticulously detailed in the Old Testament. See 1 Kings 5-8.

[4] Matthew 24:3-5 MSG

[5] Matthew 24:6-14 MSG

[6] Matthew 24:15-38, 44 MSG

[7] Matthew 24:33-34, 36; Mark 13:29-30, 32

[8] Matthew 24:42, 44

[9] For more information, visit: http://www.opendoorsusa.org.

[10] Matthew 24:6, 13 MSG

[11] 2 Timothy 1:7

[12] John 3:16-17

[13] 2 Peter 3:8-10a

[14] I highly recommend *Jerusalem: The Biography* by Simon Sebag Montefiore. It talks about how many times Jerusalem has been conquered, why people wanted to conquer it, and what it has done to one empire after another.

[15] Zechariah 12:3

[16] Avila, Jim. "Jesus of Suburbia—Has He Risen Again in Houston, Texas?" *abcnews.go.com.* ABC News Internet Ventures, March 6, 2007. http://abcnews.go.com/Primetime/story?id=2925021. See also: Wikipedia contributors. "José Luis de Jesús." *Wikipedia, The Free Encyclopedia.* Wikipedia, The Free Encyclopedia, Jan. 8, 2017.

[17] Daniel 11

[18] 2 Thessalonians 2:4

[19] Mark 13:26-27; Luke 17:34-35

WHO

[1] Daniel 9:20-23

[2] Matthew 22:9-10

[3] Matthew 5:13-15

[4] "Endgame." *Vocabulary.com.* New York: Thinkmap, Inc., 1998-2017.

[5] Daniel 9:24-27

[6] Daniel 11: 21-24, 30b, 32-37

[7] John 14:6

[8] Matthew 24:12

WHOLE NEW WORLD

[1] Psalm 33:13

[2] Mark 16:19

[3] Acts 1:11

[4] Philippians 1:22-23

[5] Luke 23:42-43

[6] John 14:2

[7] Hebrews 11:10

[8] Hebrews 11:16

[9] Revelation 21:1a

[10] Revelation 21:1b

[11] Winchester, Simon. *Atlantic: Great Sea Battles, Heroic Discoveries, Titanic Storms,* and *a Vast Ocean of a Million Stories.* New York: HarperCollins, 2010. *Pacific: Silicon Chips and Surfboards, Coral Reefs and Atom Bombs, Brutal Dictators, Fading Empires, and the Coming Collision of the World's Superpower.* New York: HarperCollins, 2015.

[12] Revelation 21:4b-6a

[13] 2 Corinthians 5:17

[14] 1 Corinthians 15:35-55

[15] 1 Corinthians 13:12-13

[16] Matthew 17; Mark 9

[17] Revelation 21:3-4, 6b-7

[18] Revelation 21:1-2, 11-14, 18-26

[19] Deuteronomy 30:11-14, 19-20

[20] Psalm 111:10; Proverbs 2:6, 9:10; Ephesians 1:8; Colossians 2:3

[21] Philippians 3:20

[22] John 14:6

WHAT NOW

[1] I confess to some ESPN as well. And I have grown kids and on-trend friends who make sure I see a respectable number of current movies and/or concerts.

[2] Does this make me sound like an arrogant intellectual? I hope not. I learn in part because I love learning, but also because I believe teaching for a living goes hand in hand with lifelong learning. Since you've invested your time in reading what I write, I owe you the best, most thoughtful information I can put on the page.

[3] Revelation 1:3; Matthew 24:15; Luke 12:37-38

[4] 2 Timothy 3:16-17

[5] 1 Peter 3:15

[6] 2 Timothy 2:15 TLB

[7] John 16:13

[8] Laurie, Greg. "Message from series 'Book of Revelation.'" *Harvest Webcasts.* Harvest Ministries, n.d. Web. http://www.harvest.org/media/webcast-series/book-of-revelation.html.

[9] Rosenberg, Joel C. *Joel C. Rosenberg's Blog.* https://flashtrafficblog.

wordpress.com. Word Press.

[10] Bilezikian, Gilbert. *Christianity 101.* Grand Rapids: Zondervan Publishing House, 1993.

[11] Stewart, Don. *The Rapture.* San Dimas: Educating Our World, 2016. Stewart, Don. *The Final Antichrist.* San Dimas: Educating Our World, 2016.

[12] Courson, Jon. *Jon Courson's Application Commentary: New Testament.* Nashville: Thomas Nelson, 2004.

[13] Boyd, Dr. Gregory. Boyd, Edward. *Letters from a Skeptic: A Son Wrestles with His Father's Questions about Christianity.* Colorado Springs: Cook Communications Ministries, 2003.

[14] Matthew 24:42, 44

[15] "Alliance." *OED Online.* Oxford University Press, Apr. 2017.

[16] See Ezekiel 38:1-6; Daniel 2:40-43; 7:7-8, 19-25; Revelation 17:3, 7, 12-17

[17] Psalm 122:6

[18] Matthew 6:10

[19] "Allegiance." *OED Online.* Oxford University Press, Apr. 2017.

[20] Mark 16:15

[21] "Distress." *Merriam-Webster.com.* Merriam-Webster, n.d. Apr. 2017.

[22] Matthew 16:15; Mark 8:29; Luke 9:20

[23] Luke 9:23-27

[24] Awana (an acronym of "Approved Workmen Are Not Ashamed," the first five words of 2 Timothy 2:15) is an international evangelical Christian nonprofit organization founded in 1950, that provides curriculum and program resources for weekly clubs for children and youth. https://www.awana.org/

[25] Promise Keepers is a Christ-centered nonprofit founded in 1990 by Bill McCartney, dedicated to motivating men to influence their world through a relationship with Jesus Christ.
https: promisekeepers.org/

[26] John 16:8; 4:35-37

Q & A

[1] Mark 4:24-25

[2] 2 Thessalonians 2:7

[3] Morris, Edmund. *Dutch: A Memoir of Ronald Reagan.* New York: Random House, 1999.

[4] Proverbs 12:10

[5] Psalm 36:5-6

[6] Isaiah 11:6, 65:5

[7] Exodus 9:12; 10:1, 20; 11:10; 14:8 NIV

[8] Romans 1:18-32 NIV

[9] Thompson, Francis. "The Hound of Heaven," London: Burns Oates & Washbourne, 1928.

Dean Curry is a husband, father, pastor, friend, and student of all things Jesus—past, present, and future.

Instagram: @deancurry

Facebook: @deangcurry

Twitter: @DeanCurry

www.ingramcontent.com/pod-product-compliance
Lightning Source LLC
LaVergne TN
LVHW051749080426
835511LV00018B/3278